Wanderings
of a Wayward
Heart

Ponderings of a
Well found Soul

Order this book online at www.trafford.com
or email orders@trafford.com

Most Trafford titles are also available at major online book retailers.

Printed in Victoria, BC, Canada.

ISBN: 978-1-4251-7401-9

*Our mission is to efficiently provide the world's finest, most comprehensive
book publishing service, enabling every author to experience success.
To find out how to publish your book, your way, and have it available
worldwide, visit us online at www.trafford.com*

Trafford rev. 1/20/2010

 www.trafford.com

North America & international
toll-free: 1 888 232 4444 (USA & Canada)
phone: 250 383 6864 ♦ fax: 812 355 4082

This book is dedicated to
Chad and Jason
I love you with all my heart.

Contents

Wanderings

This book contains a good bit of me and life as I've known it. It's been written intermittently through these years from the time I was quite young up through today. I have included things from the various ups and downs through the years to serve as a portal of sorts, to let others see things from my side of life.
I've not placed them into any particular order, just like my life. Things have happened and I've just lived along beside those things as they come.

Some of what you read here just may not be considered book worthy at all, but it's here because I felt it needed to be included for whatever reason. A few offerings here may seem quite juvenile, and that's because an undeveloped young person penned them. Others may be quite readable and possibly even enjoyable or enlightening. I hope there's more of those here than the aforementioned.

To even have a completed book is quite the little miracle to me. The one who found it pure luck to have even graduated from High School. The one that was sort of lost a good deal of life, and really never did learn much from school, or have a teacher that would give me the time of day or help in anyway. There will be enough grammatical errors and punctuation issues (especially punctuation) to make even the most lackadaisical English teacher grimace. I'm sure! My dear Aunt Setzie would have been very disappointed, I know! And I have a tendency to make up my own words. Something I've always done in life. I hope these things are less a detriment and more what makes it a curious read for you. Some may end up shaking their heads and asking, "However did this woman manage to get a book published?"

Ponderings

As a matter of fact, not too much about this book may end up being what one might consider proper or maybe even the least bit good or interesting. It's not really meant to be. It just is what it is. It's only me, written all over the place and exposed now for your voyeuristic curiosity into what I'm all about. It may surprise some, disappoint others, and just end up in the 'not so significant' discard pile of still others. In all actuality, I wrote this for my boys. So that long after I am gone from planet earth, they might have something tangible to pick up and hold as a small piece of their mom. Something I wish that I'd had from my own mom through the years. To leave a small legacy, and to include just a tiny bit of who I really am and where I've come from in life. I would like to believe that my doing this will mean something significant to them at some point in time.

And if you were kind enough to check this book out, I hope you'll get to take something from it as well. I hope you'll find it worthy of your time and effort by some small measure. And that you can look past the mistakes, errors, and just plain boring stuff, to see the underlying soul of it.

Things lie herein from my life, long forgiven and forgotten. There are lessons learned, insights gained, people who shaped my thoughts and influenced me for the better (or sometimes worse). A few bad experiences for sure, but also many blessings that I could account for and record as well. All in the form of well ordered verse and thoughts and feelings shared.

Regardless, thanks for reading one woman's life story in the bits and pieces that have been compiled into this one place of wandering through the years.

God Bless You,
linda

Stirrings

This heart
and it's wanderings just can not
be stilled.
Can never stay at home where it
belongs. Always meandering,
always dreaming.
So out of character
and out of sync.
Where it will take me
can not be foretold, and
even so, I would never tell
if I knew.
For the far off places,
out of reach spaces can not
be approached, but are
deeply longed for...desired.
And the roving heart
just won't be stilled.
Never at rest and never
at home where it belongs.
But always longing, aching,
pining away,
and passionately waiting
for some small spark of life to possess.
Does it exist?
Or is there just a glimpse, a flicker of
hope for a small ray of happiness dwelling
"out there somewhere" just beyond reach?
A semblance of peace in a troubled world,
or merely a distant and cold lonely planet
where this wandering heart
just can't be
stilled.

Searchlight

Kindred searcher
trekking the world.
Seeking, always seeking.
Will your heart never be at peace?
What or who is it that you search for
that can not be found by simply
standing still
and listening?
Quietly.
To what your heart
already knows.
That He is real.
That it is He that searches for you.
With endless stirrings of the soul,
the heart just will not be satisfied until you
ask Him in. And so,
patiently He awaits.
Standing at the ready to take you in,
to give you rest
at the end of your journey.
O weary traveler,
even if the road's end
is named
ruin.

•

Isaiah 42:16
The Lord will turn the darkness before you
into light, the rough places into level ground.
These are the things He will do,
and He will never forsake you.

You Matter

Life is about change.
Leaves changing colors in the fall,
the sky from blue to gray.
The day from sun to shadow.
Season's, the ongoing metamorphous.
The dying back, to again in spring bring forth
budding new life.
In a blink we see how the spark of summer becomes
the hush of winter snows.

People change as well. The loving people we
cherish can all too soon,
in an instant, become a distant memory
of our past. Who we were,
what we did, our dreams, hopes and goals
can all change...and most often do.

If nothing else, we are all about change.
As you go through this changing life, the one thing you need
always remember is that there is but one constant.
One thing that will never change. And that is the fact that
you are greatly loved.
Through all the storms, the thunderous and rainy times life brings, the bad
and even in the beautiful sunny days as well. The challenges come and then
they're gone.
The many ups and downs that have brought you to where you are today all
speak the same language, when they bring you to this one thing.
This one truth that always
remains the same. You are loved. God loves you, and so do I.
You have made a difference in my life.

And I just wanted you to know that today.

•

I thank my God upon every remembrance of you. Phl 1:3

3

The Painting

(for Jerry)

If I could paint a lovely picture
of the years shared in our life,
I'd surely use the brightest colors
to portray my role as wife.

I'd add brightly blooming flowers
and butterflies and such,
and the laughter that you've given me
would add a special touch.

There are no colors that could portray
the love that we have shared.
There are no words to rightly express
those loving ways you've always cared.
I love you more than life itself.
And pray for you each day.
You are my knight in shining armor,
the sunshine in my day.

In all these years together
the greatest joys I've ever known,
are the days we've had together,
the love you've always shown.

Even though our picture isn't perfect,
it's still a lovely work of art!

He's only one guy in a million. Nothing outstanding you
see. But he's just got something...can't name it, that makes him
special to me. His actions aren't that amazing, his talents are
somewhat few. But he does so much I appreciate and cheers me when
I feel blue. He's quite awkward when it comes to some things, but he
does the best that he can. No one fully knows the love that I share
with this "one guy in a million man." 1976

4

Tiny Dreamer

Sleepy boy, little one.
You have left our hearts undone.
With dreams of kitties and puppies and things,
and wide-eyed wonder of butterfly wings.
God whispers your name
and you laugh right out loud.
You spy clusters of cherubs
adrift on a cloud.
All the world's wonder,
all of heaven's joy,
are wrapped up in the fancies
of this cherished boy.

•

Youth

Little boy upon the sand,
you look at the world with eyes that search.
You're content in your land of dreams.
What do you find across the sea?
A phantom ship, a wind that sings?
Look!
There's a seashell.
It looks at me and I look at you.
Silly little one,
you go laugh and play.
There's a whole lifetime ahead of you

This piece (Youth) is the very first thing I ever remember
writing in my life. I don't know if it really is the first, but
it's about as far back as I can remember, so it's pretty old.

5

Love X Two

My one little boy has eyes of greenish blue. He's ornery as they come,
but he's an angel too.
His hazel eyed little brother is even more ornery yet! But I'd trade
them for none other, on that you can surely bet!
They brighten my day more than anyone.
With their smiles and giggles and tricks. They're kind and good and
very smart, for their wee ages of eight and six. Yes, the both of them
are quite a pair. My two rag muffins with mussed up hair.
A dirty face, an untied shoe,
and all the love in the whole wide world
multiplied by two.
- 1977 -

To Chad and Jason with all my love.
All of my hopes and dreams,
all of my earthly joys.
Tied into two small bundles
and would not be
without those boys!

What Matters

It's life...
simple and unembelished
with things that really don't matter.
The fleeting moments of beauty
in flower petals, sand on the beach,
and white clouds against
brilliant blue backdrops.
It's time, stood still.
In the first infant breath taken in
and in the last living breath
let out,
of one that is your entire
world and all.
It is majestic.
And it is at
this very moment,
fragile.
So live life well,
lest it fall to the ground
petal by petal,
covering your world
with what could have
been.

•

Minute by minute - hour by hour,
elusive life scatters with the wind.

Favored

Thank you Lord.
You have given me so much.
You have allowed the pins to be
knocked right out from under me,
then picked me up to stand
once again.
I have owned love, life, and happiness,
and lost everything I ever thought I knew,
to then have been restored joy.
How simple,
this complicated life.
For all the good and all the bad have come
and gone with you there
interested,
and concerned enough to not let me
totally flounder while
"going it on my own."
Only now to arrive at this place.
To know that the love You've always offered
is not dependent upon whether
I'm good or not.
Whether I'm there or not.
And really has nothing to do with me at all.
All I have to do is know you love me
enough.
To "stick it out" through my
roller coaster, thrill-seeking, self-serving,
constantly searching for something more life,
and yet not hold it against me.

If I had a best friend of flesh and bones
that had been treated as I have you,
continuously pushed and pulled,
shamefully ignored, verbally abused,
taken for granted, gone uncared about,
or not given the time of day, or listened to...
who had seen me behave in most shameful
unbecoming ways that shocked and confounded,
they then most certainly would have left me
in my state of freely chosen oblivion long ago.
But yet here you are.
Still willing to love me well into my next
crisis of wrong choices made.
For helping me grow,
allowing the growing pains,
for just loving me through
and not abandoning me...Lord,
I profoundly thank you.

September 1999

Ageless Thanks

Love has touched the wrinkled brow.
The leathery palm of this hand.
I've worked these years in gratitude
for the beautiful, bountiful land.
The Lord my God sustained me.
Through good times, and through
the bad.
I'll thank Him and praise His holy name,
for the wonderful blessings I've had.

The Dark

Darkness comes in many ways.
It follows you throughout your days.
Evening comes and with the night,
creeping shadows, sheltered light.
Reach out for meaning
life insists.
Or you'll fade like the darkness,
deep into mists.
- 1963 -

Brevity

My youth is spent like gold dust scattered in the wind, so fleeting.
And all the beauty lived therein, captured as notes played upon ivory
keys, which have since floated into space toward ears untrained to
hear them, and now forever played.
When life is defined by four-walled confines within the mind's
corridors, and there are no risks taken, no true passions lived,
then unrest is become a familiar companion to life.

And life itself a mere stepping stone toward higher eternal things.
But all of life's glances backward can n'er be seen as gain.
If you've never made love count
in the heart of
even
one.

Who Is The Author?

Whose heart is this?
Bleeding all over the pages
of this book?
Is it yours?
How very rude
just to let it all spill out this way
for all the world to see.
Not even bothering to mop it up
or try to remove the stain.
But oh no, here it is
wrung out upon this white parchment
so that those who read it's lines
can all feel a bit queasy at it's viewing.
Someone's dripped it out in fragmented
words and phrases while it's still beating!
Can you imagine that?
Spatters from careless, thoughtless
acts of life which now pool into thickly clotted
and scattered ramblings throughout.
Pain almost oft' it's precursor, continuously
pricking it all the way.
So what's to be done now with such a sight as this?
Tear out the besmudged pages and begin again?
Leave them as a timeless measure for more additions
later on? Or...add to them the wash of tears from years of
searching, which help to cleanse the soul
and the pages of this book called - Life?

(And just where has the author gone anyway?)

She Took Me In

When the world shifted off it's axis and tipped my balance to then knock me out from under any true sense of reality; and there didn't seem to be a soft place to land or anyone on God's green earth who cared, she took me in.

When neat and tidy lives did not care to be disrupted for the likes of a lost and scraggly misplaced and undone girl of fifteen, she opened her life to disruption and chance and took me in.

No one could really ever know what life looks like from the inside looking out at age fifteen with no parents, and nothing that encompasses your life to reassure you that you matter to someone, anyone...or even to just ONE person out there.
I was not incorrigible, or wayward, or delinquent, I was unwanted.

And I was too young to be without a mom who had died, and a dad who didn't care but only just enough to see that I was "out of his way," so that he could get on to live his life of choice. He wished to move on...without me.

Lost does not begin to describe what life was about to a young teenager who was in such need, yet ignored and passed over so completely. And no one could ever fathom the depths of gratitude from the chance I was given at my lowest point in life, just because...she took me in.

There was so little of life worth clinging to then. And no direction or guides to steer the paths ahead of me. But only a place to lay my head and a determination to try to live the best that I could in alien surroundings that were filled with people I barely knew at all.

I was eight years old before I discovered that this woman had the title of 'sister' to me. I remember thinking how very strange that was; to have a sister that I didn't know was my sister, that I really didn't know very well at all. I'd seen her often enough, played with her son (who was almost my age), as a playmate now and again, and I'd seen her tend to her other children, but my sister? What a startling revelation for an eight year old to have!

Whatever the paths that crossed, the battles fought, victories and defeats that came, this woman so familiar that I'd hardly known, became unwilling at some point to let me get completely lost along the way. And although life's journeying was difficult and long, and there had been many detours and road blocks taking varied routes along the way through the years, I was able to make it and still come out whole and complete today only because, she took me in.

My crime in life had been losing my mother to death, and my father to selfish unconcern, and being a matter of nothing more than an inconvenience left behind for others to deal with. I had never once been asked if I was all right after my mothers death, or if I just needed to come stay with anyone for a little while just to make sure things were ok and see to it that I could grieve as the still child that I was then. No teacher that offered counseling or concern, or one person that even offered a hug of comfort to me for the rampant grief and feeling of displacement run amok inside of me to the point that I thought that I might burst at the seams.

Security that I desperately needed was gone. And so too seemed any hope, as I tried to cope on my own. An adolescent with no one to turn to, which easily could almost have become a lifelong struggle, a constant searching to fill the gaping holes left in the heart from lack and unconcern.

And when no one else wanted me around or knew just how to take care of the problem of "what to do with linda" (the girl no one wanted), after it had become all too evident that her father didn't want her either, she...took me in.

For allowing me in, and for caring for such an unwanted stick of a girl in life who came with no guarantees, I am forever grateful. I will always be grateful to the "sister I didn't know," for not allowing me to flounder. Or to be tossed aside or shoved out into the restless sea of uncertainties to be completely lost or drowned without being given another thought.
Loving gratitude for giving me a place, despite the hardships it may have caused her life and the lives of her own family (to whom I am also very grateful).

I'm glad that I didn't become the common afterthought that so many in life do in other such unfortunate circumstances. You know, like the one that you hear that asks, "I wonder whatever became of __?__ and nobody really ever knows?"
All because I was given a second thought. And a chance to finish growing, and some of the attention needed as an undeveloped and not yet done young person in great need. I became who I am now in life...a whole person. A wife and mom of two of my own children, a writer, an astute observationist of life. Confident and strong and not too shabby a person to know once you really try to get to know me.
I just needed a chance to finish growing up well.
One person seemed to care enough about me so that I could.
That one person was named Carolyn, and she's my sister.
And I will forever be grateful to and respect her for opening her life and her heart when I needed it most.
And just because, she took me in.

And my prayer for her is that Jesus, you would always be there for her in life. Because you love her, and just because...You took her in.

Mama's Things

At the end of her life, all of the things I had left of mama could fit inside a small canvas tote bag. Some of her poetry (included in this book), a handful of pictures, a pretty and delicate fall leafed cotton handkerchief with a white sugar cube that was hand decorated with a tiny pink pansy atop it, the old poetry book she used to read to me from when I was a little girl.
I remembered that mama had especially saved the sugar cube from one of the ladies "fancy church luncheons" that she'd attended, and more than likely helped to plan.
I remember that mama was 'the music' portion of this and so many other functions through the years.
She was 'the music' one year in a Christmas program in my grade school. It was the year that a girl in my class, Donna Miller, I think her name was, fainted onstage when we were standing up there practicing our song. We had to wait, including mama, until Donna was properly revived and led off stage, before continuing.

Inside that bag are desperate cherished memories that the heart is sometimes not strong enough to hold. The mind scrambles to assemble them quickly, furiously fitting one upon another. Trying to build a lifetime on.
A handful of precious possessions meaningful only to me.
The small brown covered book of poetry, 'Songs Of The Treetop And Meadow,' it's pages tattered and yellowed and falling out from time's wear and tear, ready to crumble at the mere touch. I had laid across sideways on mama's bed for hours as she read that book to me. How thankful I am that it somehow made it's way inside this bag.

I close my eyes, and the projector begins to play.
There's mama, sitting at her pink and gray and white flecked piano. (Yes it really was that color, painted lovingly by her to match the rest of her decor in the living room). Quite the colorful canvas.

She's wearing what I refer to as "that serious kind of little smile" she would always get when she was immersed in her music. And she would often be singing, lost in a peaceful comfortable place, a world free of pain and any care.

But I also remember seeing lonely saddened eyes. I remember them vividly as well. Eyes that would spring wide with light and laughter when she'd set her fingers upon the keyboard to play. Then they just seemed to sparkle and dance. And I can see her hands glide effortlessly across the ivory keys. I see those hands so clearly. And they always had their own distinct fragrance, somewhere betwixt 'Channel No.5' and 'Evening In Paris' and the onions she'd just chopped for our evening supper.

Her hair was white.

And I couldn't honestly remember a time in my almost 15 years of growing up when it wasn't. And I remember that she never thought she was pretty. She wasn't. She was beautiful.

She died tired and worn down, haggard from fighting against an invisible monster that raged within. The cancer wore her out and robbed her life away. From her, from me. It's so hard to remember things sometimes.

And I often find that I wonder if life truly ever existed before she was taken. These tiny little "patchlets" of recalled and selective moments. Or were they merely figments of my imagination?

A girl of just barely fifteen needs her mom, and mine was forever gone from me.

My limited understanding then, could not prepare me for the repercussions of that reality. It's only now that my life aches for those two warm and loving arms to comfort in the night. To help me make it through my own grown-up struggles and faceless nameless fights. And for her ears to listen when a best friend's counsel is needed most. And fun...that only two women can share as adults who have traveled far and distant miles together on pathways all the same.

How I have missed her through these years. And missed knowing who she really was as a person. Not just the one who cooked and cleaned, washed dishes, did laundry and was there and then wasn't. Not just a wife to my dad or my mother, but a woman. With a woman's desires, dreams and passions in life. With memories all her own. Some to share, some to harbor in her heart. With a woman's wisdom to pass along to a sorely unwise daughter.

I caught but such a tiny glimpse of it then; her unique essence. And remember it now as but a faded shadow which glides across the chambers of my heart's recollections.
Somehow seeming lost, with no place to rest.

I would give all that I had to sit now with mama for just ten minutes. To be able to hold her gently and tell her things turned out all right, and to see her smile that eternal sign of understanding that she was and is still, so important to me.
So beautiful, so loved, and I didn't get to tell her just how much she meant to God, and how important she had been to so many on this tiny spinning blue sphere while she was here. Her life counted.

She was important and her life meant so much more than could ever fit into the confines of this small canvas bag. All of mama's things are valued and their worth measured without boundaries within my heart.

The world knew nothing of her secret dreams, this rare and priceless pearl left undiscovered. You can count on one hand those who caught a fleeting glimpse of her inner beauty. And those who did, recognized the treasure there and were indeed truly blessed at having known her.

The Clown

Emmett Kelley's sadness is, a constant reminder to me.
Of life's betrayal of happiness and it's joyous trickery.
You may take the worst in stride
and put on a happy face,
but deep within the hurt is there, it's left it's final trace.
Happiness is an ornament, expensive,
but not to buy.
Sadness is much more easily acquired,
but no one's
ever known why.
There's so many 'happy people'
living on just
that pretense, that if all of them were gathered, the
'joy' would be immense!
These people can't fool Emmett or me,
we can tell them apart.
Sadness is a specialty, when you're
simply playing a clown at heart.

Mom

Beloved memories unfold with
every passing day.
A lovelier lady none could behold,
but she couldn't stay.
She made such beautiful music,
and her poetry lives on still.
She may be lost to us for awhile,
but her loving warmth
never will.

In memory of my mother, Vida Marie (Setzer) Pharaoh
Gone from us may 8th, 1964

18

The accompanying letter to the poem: Mother's Garden

Dear Friends,

   I tried to come up with a Mother's Day greeting for
*P.A.C. moms, symbolic in a sense, and came up with the
various contrasts that exist within the simple rose. The velvety
smoothed petals, fragrance, the brilliantly textured and deeply
hued flower we are so familiar with and love. A true thing of
beauty to behold, and yet at times it has been known to inflict
pain from the very thorns that nourish it upon it's woody stem
onto the unsuspecting hand that would steal it away from it's
place of glory and status in the flower bed.
   And then I thought of the heart of a mother. The various
layers of love that lie therein for every child conceived from
within it's depths and boundaries, and the infinite beauty of
that love.
   Simeon aptly foretold of Mary's own "piercing of the
heart" (to the soul), as she lovingly gazed down in awe at ten
tiny fingers and toes and the wide promising eyes, so trusting
and bright, that gazed back at her.

   No trace of thorns there.

   So amidst the beauty and love, awe and wonder,
beyond the dreams and longings of our souls, and in the
center of the deep bond of love we share with our beloved
children...come thorns.
   We are indeed mothers who have most closely
identified with a loving heavenly Father in the most intimate
and personal way, through pain. And the shared love of our
sons and daughters.

We may have carried them near our hearts for nine months, anxiously awaited their arrival, each one...and knew and loved them beyond comprehension the moment of conception and before we saw their smiling little faces, held their tiny hands in ours, saw them take their first step, or sit for the first time in their new clothes in a new desk at a new school, away from us for the very first time, but we carry them in our hearts a lifetime.

Away from us then seemed almost too much to bear. And we've since stood and watched them grow and go onto pathways fraught with danger and perilous things. Yes we've been pricked by the thorns. And instead of just wishing you all a "Happy Mother's Day" today, although you well deserve such a wish, I wrote you a poem.

And I would like to just tell you what a very special person you are, and that God loves you dearly, and has seen your noble work of motherhood (mistakes and all), and will answer the prayers of your mother's heart.

He too has suffered a great deal as a loving parent. He above anyone else, can understand and reach down and heal the thorn pricked bleeding heart wounds we have suffered, and wipe away the countless tears shed on behalf of our children, and give us strength and hope for each new day.

My prayer for you is that each new day will find your heart filled more with the beauty of the rose than the thorns. And may God bless you today on this Mother's Day. Especially with His love and peace where your children are concerned.

From one mom to another in loving friendship, Lin

*PAC (Parents of Adult Children) A class started in our (then) church.

●

Of love, life, and laughter three...two words prevail,
"encourage me."

Mother's Garden

There are thorns among the roses
as every mother knows.
From one tiny dependent living beauty, to wherever
innocence goes.
There are prickly hurts and thorny aches along the pathways
of motherhood. And beauteous, loving, wonderful flowers,
which in mother's hearts are all good.
In every flower garden the regal rose doth reign. A thing of
unspeakable joy and beauty, not viewed an instrument of pain.
As in every mother's heart, so our children seem. Royal and
regal in beauty and love, a woman's fondest dream.
And walking in the garden of life, as we pluck the rose so
bold, sometimes the thorns do make us bleed, for their beauty
we long to hold.
So tread lightly in your "mother's garden" and regard each
flower with care. For with every fragrant lovely rose are
thorns placed here and there.
But which of us could ever stop loving those wondrous regal
things? Or cease to touch their unmatched beauty, or refuse the
joys they bring?
God the tender gardener, of roses given into our care, can
make them blossom and unfold, when we go walking there.
And remember it's Him who gave them, and with them
entrusts us still.
With every thorn upon every rose, they're tended each at His
will. So mother's hearts take comfort, and enjoy each rose as
you may. And let God have all the thorns, which prick and
hurt along the way. Yes there's thorns among the roses, as
every mother's heart fully knows.
But who would trade a single petal, of a
God tended, mother loved, blooming rose?

(written and given to P.A.C. (parents of adult children) moms
at Bethel, Mother's Day - 5/10/96)

Mother's Day Poem

(sent to all the moms in my address book for
mother's day, May 10, 2009)

It seems like only yesterday
we held their hands so small.
Then turned for just a moment's time...
When did they get so tall?

We used to pick them up with ease,
Caress their tears away.
In our Mother's hearts now older,
it will always stay that way.

We may no longer carry them lovingly,
to tuck them in their beds.
We may no longer soothe away their pain
or worry from their heads.

But they surely will be covered,
with the love that's been there from the start.
Blanketed safely with our earnest prayers,
and kept safe and close within our hearts.

A mother's love will never end.
Her duties never waver.
Here's to all the years you've worked so hard
gathering memories to savor.

Happy Mother's Day

May your Mother's Day Be Especially Blessed!

Embraced

He is but a mist in a dream.
So far removed
that the memory betrays the mind.
Tricks the heart into thinking
He was never really there at all.

Oh, but he was.
And I never really knew him.
For he gathered all that is him
into the hidden shelter of the heart,
and would not let me in.

Oh, how I long for a dance in shadow land
that would reveal his troubled heart.
So that I might become the sunlight,
to chase off all the darkness.

But the soul within me weeps from lack.
Knowing that I'll not be the one
who'll lead him into brighter places,
who will illumine his way.

For his life is held within the grasp of
more loving hands than these that are mine.
And will see him home.
And will see him home.

For my Michael, my heart

The Phone Call

He said, "I am in great need and troubled."
She felt the elastic band around her heart tighten.
He said, "I have no home to call my own."
She knew "home" was in one's heart.
He seemed so urgent,
so desperate and needy and...
she cried.
Who was this lost soul that had come
into the world so innocently?
Who once began life so new and filled with
promise? This shadow drifting
like an unseen mist through
the chambers of her heart?
The very thought of his words just now spoken,
made her soul so cold. A cold that made her ache
to the very core of her being.
In a sea of thousands, he seemed so lost.
Will he ever find the truth?
Mother's hearts must be made of elastic you see,
to stretch to the very point of break.
She tries to think, but it's as if she's forgotten
how.
The sting of pain...his,
is just too great to keep a rational thought
in place. There are but five words that come to mind.
That reverberate into the boundless universe and echo
the halls of heaven as a heart wrenching prayer...
A mother's cry, "Please Lord,
don't forget him."

The Mark

You are inscribed in the palms
of His hands.
Reject Him if you will.
But proof of His love for you stands.
You can not take a big eraser
and rub it out.
The wounds are deep,
all the way through...complete.
Some wounds are like that.
When love wounds it's permanent.
Fixed for all time and space.
And nothing can ever change it.
This you've known from long ago.
Mere life can not change it, nor
can you.
You may try to reject.
You may try to forget.
But,
you are inscribed in
the palms of His
hands.
- for cm -

•

If every grain of sand was obliterated,
there would be no beautiful beaches.
Nothing to adorn or compliment the seas.
Don't allow the puny circumstances of life,
no matter how difficult, to steal even one grain
of the sand of your true self worth. - lmpc

Beloved Ghost

He glides through hallways with efficacy, silent and aloof.
Peering down upon those of the living as he makes his way.
He goes from here...to over there, and there is no destination
for his wanderings.
He is merely a shadow of the one he was, and one can not hold
a shadow close or soothe it with a warm embrace. You reach
out for them, and they're not there.
So stilled a heart that beat so full of life, which fed the soul and
created dreams of long ago. So very...long ago.
We are only the visited, nothing more.
Graced with the presence of a ghostly apparition in human
form which once was called "son."
We passionately desire the deepest connection to those who
are mere vapors that surround us. The longing for closeness in
the forbidden enclaves of their souls.
Where emotion romps freely and doesn't ever stop to wonder
or question it's intent.
Shadows and ghosts are good at hiding. We know they are
with us and sense them near. And yet you try to clasp their
hand and find they are not really there at all.
And who is this spirit so familiar?
The name known to me for so long does not now
fit the frame.
Distant but close...I witness the evolution of this one we love
so well, as he glides effortlessly from our lives.

●

Having a child hide from you as a parent, can break your
heart. There are no words to describe losing a child. Physically
or emotionally. And when you're exceptionally close as a
family, it can really pull you through some strange enough
knot holes. Hold your dear ones close. Nothing is worse than
not having those you love best in your life. And nothing in
heaven or earth should be worth such heartache. Especially
when you have the power to do something about it.

The Prodigal Way

I never thought the road would be so long Lord.
I didn't know I'd be traveling alone.
For only the heart of a searching mother
could be compelled to go down this roadway
toward a child that's lost.
In my mind's eye he is not grown.
In my heart I do not see the young woman
ready to face the harsh realities of life.
They are toddlers
tottering through a lion's den,
and the lion's are hungry.
Yes, they choose their way, but Lord...you
know it's impossible to see the right way to go
when all is dark around you.

Please...
pierce their vision with your light!
Even the thinnest shaft of your brightness
may be enough to cause them to turn
in the right direction.
Until that time, I wait and pray.
And watch and trust.
And hope with every fiber of my being
that I'll meet them on the road halfway.
For it's then I'll know
when I see (his) face,
he's coming home
to stay.

This Song Remembered

There...I thought I saw him standing.
For a moment, in a blink.
In the shadows of the evening moonlight
which lit the darkened room where peacefully I sat.
An old familiarity to quickly prod my memory
of days spent, and snap shots taken in my mind and stored
within my heart.

I can see him in the quiet times,
and often hear him in music being offered.
Taking me back to a simpler life and happier times.
He walks daily upon my heart. And there are times that
the footsteps are heavier than at others,
which cause this mother's heart pain.
But mostly, they're light and fanciful.
Revealing the little boy I love so much.
Shadows...shadows...shadows.
Tis' only this I see.
If I could, I'd mold them into reality. Into the one that I
would hold close for a time. Into the one that God designed.
He stands before me not in heart shadows, but radiant moon
beams dancing in my soul. I enter into the celebration that is
my son.
Now, I simply close my eyes, sit back and "see" him sitting
there. At the old piano that he used to play. A beautiful song
that I hear drifts from some boxed music source.
But for me, it's his fingers making the melody that I hear,
and I'm longing for his music.

The power of it's messages known only to him. The softness of
those soothing chords that welled up from deep within his
soul, now broken by time and circumstance.
Oh, how I miss you my boy.
You'll never know.

How I long for the you that was left here behind.
The strong independent thinker. The filibuster of profound
ideals for any ear that would listen. How strong and quick
your mind. How gifted God made you to be.
And...I profoundly miss you.

The ivory keys now lay blanketed in dust underneath a cover
never opened. The silence almost too much to bear,
overwhelming me with such a sense of loss. I pray that God
will revive your heart, your soul, and that you'll emerge the
wonder He created. The undiscovered lost symphony yet to be
played. His masterpiece to the world. Which will bring it to
it's feet with applause.

I miss you my son. And the beautiful music that is you.
And I love you with all of my heart. I hope you'll one day
know just how much.
Maybe when heaven is home and you're playing once again.
Making your wonderful music, with me listening along with
the angel choirs.
You are my beloved son in whom I am well pleased and
tonight,
I especially miss you.

•

Philemon 1:15 "For perhaps he was for this reason
parted *from you* for awhile, that you should
have him back forever.

Dad In A Box

How strange.
Sitting cross-legged on the floor in the center of this darkened room...sifting.
Piece by piece, bit by bit, connecting the dots, assembling the puzzle, counting the signs left behind in a pile no bigger than what would fit into an old tack box.
Some scribbled words jotted on this scrap of paper or that, and pictures.
Old, faded, all black and white, brown and beige and surprisingly, some of me.
Surprising, considering that this man had been detached and unavailable to me for so many years. And now...
here I sit. Pouring over every tiny spec of life I can get my hands onto. Trying so hard to find even the smallest spark of reality. A validation of sorts that I am indeed connected somewhere.

There's a crayon drawn picture with my name in childhood scrawl across the bottom inscribed, "to daddy." It appears this daddy is holding a little girl who's crying from having fallen off her tricycle.
Is that how I saw you then? My ultimate protector from all harm?
A relic saved through all these years by someone I hardly knew at all.
I must have meant something to this stranger if he'd saved it this long, don't you think? How little time we have on earth to impart the importance of love.
Some have in excess of seventy years, and still fail.
What manner of man was this to never have accomplished this in life? Not to be able to extend his heart in this simple way? And yet, here lies proof that these things must have mattered.
At least sometime in the span of life he lived.

Trying to make sense of it all.
These scraps of vague intimation from some long and distant place
seems an exercise in futility, at the very least.
And still they're here. Like silent monuments of some ancient
civilization one must excavate and explore.

Did I matter?
There are snippets of confirmation that at some point I did.
Did he matter? He brought me life then cut me loose to make it on
my own. I'm here now, so it must mean that he did.

Did we have a chance?
We missed our chances in life. Words left unsaid, love withheld,
lives undone and unraveled. Nothing but loose ends.

And all of this boiled down to cold and meaningless pictures and
'things' with lifeless faces and tidbits of unfamiliar places.
Left to summon up a ghost life from the past.
A life that fits smartly

...into dad's old tack box.

•

The most grievous wound comes not
from any weapon forged from the hand of man.
But is instead, that of a self-inflicted nature.
A result of the love that we withhold
from others. - lmpc/1999

Missing Mom

The other day as I stood at the counter making last minute preparations for our Easter Dinner, a photo flashed upon the broad screen of my mind. Out of nowhere, it just popped up. It was of a little preschool girl dressed up with a very lovely multi-floral Easter bonnet, and kneeling behind her was a plump little woman also similarly adorned, but in a much more flashy chapeaux, that was probably taller than the little girl standing. It seemed to rival any 'Cat's Hat' out there as far as height, style and p'nash! She had her arms wrapped around the little girl. How strange and yet so familiar it all seemed. After all, the little girl was me. And my mom was the creator of said hats of many garnishments. She had made her own and mine that matched (except for height), to wear in the ladies annual Easter Hat Regalia, in the small town in which we lived. I can barely recall any of that time, but I do recall how much joy my mom had in participating in these events, and that the joy spilled over onto me. How wonderfully creative and talented she was.

My eyes welled up with tears for a brief moment with the words uttered under my breath, "I wish I could have known you mom." I am now 56 years old as of this year, and I have missed out on forty some years of my mother's wonderful creativity and talent. I lost her to cancer when I had barely turned 15 years of age. And so now after marrying, having two children, (grand children she never got to meet in life), and plunging headlong into senior citizens status myself as-it-were, I realize more each day just how much missing that really is.

She was just the most remarkable woman. She could hear a new song played once on the radio and go to the piano and sit down and play it beautifully!

She wrote the most wonderful poetry that I've ever read. She made things like blue ribbon Easter Parade hats (yes, she really did win a blue ribbon for that aforementioned mile-high hat), and her May baskets were second to none!

I remember mama playing accompaniment for many of our school musicals and the time that Donna Miller fainted on stage while mom, not realizing what had happened, played merrily away until someone pointed out Donna laying on the floor. And I remember the awards I received for being a big black cat once, and the Aunt Jemima costume mom had created in grade school for me at Halloween. I always won the award for the best costumes! And there were the saturday night dances in the Ogden City Hall. Mom played in the band and I danced around the floor on my dad's shoes until I got tired enough to crawl up on the coat covered chair trolleys to fall fast asleep until it was time to go home. These were all part of the memories that came flooding in like the tide there at that very moment, standing at the kitchen counter by the sink.

I was able to have these tiny bits of mom to carry me on through life, but oh what I wouldn't give to have had her standing beside me in my journey along the way. Back then I knew who she was. She was my mom. I would have loved knowing her as Marie, the beautiful talented woman with hopes and dreams of her own, the destined-for-great-things-that-could-have-been-if-only-person, that she was. I could have learned so much more from this fascinating woman that gave me life.

I loved her then and love her memory now. Only now I maybe sorta, kinda, just might know her better since I have ALL these years of womanly wisdom racked up to my credit. And I write this just to let someone know what an important influence this woman, Vida Marie (Setzer) Pharaoh, has had in my life through these many years. Even in her absence, she's been there for me through these memories.

I used to look up at the stars and think of them as the households of heaven. And that the light that came from within each one was someone's loved one up there cleaning and making ready the rooms for all of those who would "come home soon" to be with them.

I just knew that my 'mom's house' was the one that sparkled brightest in the moonlit sky as she prepared our rooms and all of our special things for us. She was up there taking all the great care that she put in that little girl's Easter Bonnet, into welcoming her family back to her one day.

And today, in the bright evening starlight, these 56 year old eyes still look heavenward and see "mom's place" sparkle with that welcoming light. And I can tell that it is going to be such a wonderful reunion one day. We will have over 40 years to catch up on after all. And who knows? She just may be wearing one of her wonderful Easter Bonnets when I get there!

•

Why am I here?
Have you ever wondered that?

Well...
If you caused a smile
and not a frown.
Lifted someone up when
they were down.
Helped turn a woeful heart around,
then you'll know why God
keeps you around.
04/07

From An Angel

God heard it from an angel, your every hurt and fear.
For she sat and listened lovingly, and counted every tear.
Not one concern escaped her, attentively she heard.
Even the unspoken pains, too much for just mere words.
For He Himself appointed this special one to care.
Who from her depths of love for you...would all your burdens bear.
In life her name was "Grandma." Her love...like His, failed never!
To be there when you need to share, and love you for forever.
Yes, God heard it from an angel, the depths of time and space
transcend. For such a great and loving task, just who else would He
send?

To make sure that you know He's there, to wrap you up in love.
He sent a special angel from eternity above. And you can know she's
told Him, your every heart's concern and need...for this angel
especially loves you, and on your behalf she pleads.
God heard it from an angel. From a loving grandma's eternal view.
Of a beloved grandson's trouble, his hope her desire to renew.
And perhaps the beauty of the moment will help you understand, the
special love of this messenger, a touch of her eternal loving hand.

God uses many instruments to help us feel His love. This time He
sent a special one, to you from heaven above. And rest assured He'll
listen to every word she has to say. For every word is hemmed in
love to speed it on it's way. So when the cares of this hard world,
come flooding in to cause you sorrow, let His love flow freely over
you, to take you to the morrow. Your tears are always in His sight,
your lonely struggles He will heed.
His ears aren't deaf nor His eyes blind, He knows your every need.
Remember, God heard them from an angel.

September of 93' for J - who needed someone to talk to about
'things', so Grandma appeared in a dream he had, just to be able to
hear his every concern and help unburden his heart.

Katy

This is dedicated to our sweet and precious Katy Mabel Josephine Carlson. A bundle of fur that we were privileged to have with us for fifteen years of wonderful life shared. Our 'pets' are more to us than that. They are such a part of our daily lives and become so engrained in our hearts, that losing them takes a time of grieving akin to nothing else. They are there for us. Loyal, loving, undemanding treasured friends for as long as God allows them to stay. Katy is one of many of our beloved friends who have gone before us. One of my first questions to God when I get to heaven is going to be, "God, why couldn't our dear sweet furry friends live at least as long as we did while on earth?" They, from out of anyone else, deserved to live very long and lasting lives of joy.

It was early February 1994. I had just returned from a trip up north to Minnesota with some family friends to see our sons who were attending classes at Crown College. While there, our son sort of booted out the guys in his living space to accommodate 'mom' for the couple of days stay. We made a run to the grocery store and purchased a few grocery/munchie things and rented the movie 101 Dalmatians. We returned to the room and went about settling in for the evening to enjoy the movie together. At it's end, our youngest son Jason, had commented that he "wouldn't mind having another dog," he didn't think. Quite a comment from him considering it had been a full two years since we all endured the loss of our precious Patches (Patchy) as she was affectionately known by all.

A tri-colored Rat Terrier who had stolen our hearts when our boys were tiny themselves. She and they grew up together and lived a full and happy life together of seventeen years. We had just made it past her 17th birthday and Christmas.

Chad Michael was home and Jason was on Christmas break. We had all gone to bed after a wonderful Christmas when in the middle of the night we were awakened to Patchy's dreadful mournful cry.

She had suffered a heart attack and we had several hours to sit with her before the Vet opened his doors. Our oldest son and I took her over to be quietly put to rest. It was so very hard and it took a good solid couple of years to actually get to the point where we could even consider finding another companion. But that tidy little offhand comment was enough for me to set things in motion upon my return home. I had been watching the newspaper ads and sure enough, one day there it was! An ad touting black and white Rat Terrier puppies for sale, and not very far from us. So, despite the objections by my husband and being singularly-minded, I grabbed my oldest sister and off I went to seek out the communicators of said 'intent to provide a loving companion' to us.

When we arrived at the farm, we were led to the barn where we saw 'mom' and a couple of little ones in the straw right next to her. A male and a female. I picked up the little girl and thought she'd be just perfect for my little "Dalmatian Surprise." I paid the man and off we went. It was very cold and snowy out and she was a tiny little thing. When I arrived back home I thought that the thing to do would be to let her get down to do a bit of business before introducing her to dear hubby. Well, the little rascal took off like she'd been shot from a cannon, skittering atop the crusty snow lickety-split! I of course, had no recourse but to follow in hot pursuit. Only this tubby human body bundled to the hilt against the cold wasn't skittering a bit, more like laboring rather moose-like and feeling every asthmatic breath against the cold.

As I arrived at the spot at the end of her journey (under the neighbor's car across the empty lot on the corner), I thought to myself and then uttered a brief synopsis of the situation heavenward to an awaiting God's ever attuned ears.

"Oh Great!"

"God, I went against my husband's wishes to surprise our son and he'll have a regal-royal one to come home to at that!" A mom's funeral, but...a new puppy after all!"

I surmised, as I called out repeatedly, "Here, puppy, puppy, puppy," that the only way to capture my new little elusive friend was to take off my winter coat and fling it over her if she even came out at all.

It worked, and back toward home I trudged holding her in my coat, and just trying to breathe. It took awhile after arriving at home in the nice warm house to do that (breathe that is). Now, Jerry never said, "I told you so," or any such gibberish (I think he was too concerned about my expiring right in front of his eyes), and she seemed to weather the whole experience well.

She zipped all over the place like a houseafire that first night and I knew we were "in for it!" The next day I put a little collar on her and noticed that she hadn't or wouldn't move from the chair she had been doing jumping jimminies off of the night before. I waited and waited and waited...and nothing. Not a fraction of an inch did this little dynamo move. I thought to myself, "Oh no, we broke her!" It took awhile to realize that she, for whatever reason felt tethered to that chair the minute the collar went on. So off it came and she was her zippy puppy self again almost immediately.

I couldn't wait to let Jason meet his new girl. I told him he had a surprise, but he'd have to wait until he came home for spring break. I called her puppy-doodle for quite awhile, leaving the proper naming to him, after all...she was his dog. I had thought of several names she could have been named, among them 'Valentine', since it was Valentine's day when we picked her up. But the final decision would be Jason's.

Well as it happened, Jason called from school to say he was heading for Florida with friends for spring break, heading for the areas ravaged by hurricane Andrew to see if they could help.

One of the guy's Aunt and Uncle lived in Fort Meyers there, and would be putting them up part of the time.

Needless to say, it was gratifying to see these young men willing to give back, but disappointing that our little fur-bundle would have to wait for her name. I showed her pictures of Jason every day and told her "See, that's our Jason," and "You are his puppy." Toward the end of March when we knew we probably wouldn't see him until classes were over, I finally broke down and told him about her and sent a picture so he could "meet" her.

We traveled up to school, puppy in tow, to move Jason home after classes and the thing is, that silly little pup saw him out of all the others walking toward the school from his dorm with two other guys and just about leaped out of the car window to get at him.

She KNEW that was "her Jason" from the get-go! There was a deep and permanent bond from that moment on for the next fifteen years running.

We took her with us that same year when she was just yet a few months old, on a 22 hour drive trip to Alabama and Florida to see my sister and her husband. She traveled well for being so new and no bigger than a minute. She loved her excursions to the Dairy Queen for a bit of vanilla ice cream from time to time. She was so smart and playful. She minded so well, and she was as empathetic to our sad days as she was overjoyed with the good.

She LOVED birthdays and didn't care whose it was, she'd be right there helping to open their gifts. Of course she had her own, and Christmas (which was her very favorite) to open her oodles of toys and treats, but we would always tuck in a doggy treat or some cheerios or some such thing whenever we had a celebration, just so she would have something too. She got so excited!

She was our little lovey. Our life-companion, confidant, sharer of life, beloved friend. She was LOVED with a capital "L", And she will always be in our hearts.

In memory of Katy, our forever friend. With much love.

Katy Mabel Josephine Carlson (named after my grandma Kate)
Born December 22nd, 1993 - Died March 23rd, 2008 (Easter Sunday)

> You gave til' you just couldn't any more,
> That's what true loving friendship's for.
> To offer all that's inside to give,
> And help another friend to live.
>
> You were here but only a moment in time
> And we loved you from the start.
> No one could know the full impact of
> The paw prints you left on our hearts.
> We love you, Katy-doodle.

•

Heroes

I have one. (Hero, that is).

His name is Jerry and he happens to be married to me.

Now Jerry started off in life like everyone else, a common ordinary guy doing common ordinary every day things.

And I'm not certain when exactly that he arrived at super-hero status, but arrive he did. Most people probably wouldn't catch that about him right off, walking around in his mail carrier duds carrying a ton of letters, bills, magazines, catalogs and packages to deliver as he goes about his daily mail route. He racks up miles upon miles, as he makes his way through his work day.

But you see, it's after the regular eight or nine hour shift each day when one begins to notice the subtle markings of super-heroism in the man.

Maybe after a particularly dreary, wet, cold, chilly-to-the-bone day, when he comes home soaked...or possibly a bug-infested, sweltering, humid, suffocatingly-hot summer day, when people haven't been so cordial and nice and he's soaked again as he comes-through-the-door-dragging kind of day especially, that one can pick up on all the earmarks of what could be considered a real hero.

He is a veteran from Viet Nam. Earning the rank of sergeant along with medals before being turned loose by Uncle Sam. And even though coming back and re-acclimating was rough back in those days, he came out a whole person who kept and maintains yet today, a great sense of humor and sense of who he is.

He was a hunter at one time, but laid the gun down after the war in Viet Nam and has not desired to pick it up since. I know he would in a split minute if he had to defend his family, but he came away with a new respect for living and for the living things that surround him from that experience.

Jerry suffered a heart attack on the job twelve years ago. It was the worst day of my life. As I picked up the phone that day to hear a woman from the local hospital telling me to rush over there because Jerry had driven himself into the ER in his mail jeep just a few minutes earlier, and he was in trouble.

While there, I saw them wheel him out on a gurney to a life flight helicopter for transfer to one of the larger hospitals, stop midway and return because he died on the tarmac and they needed to bring him back in to resuscitate and stabilize him for transport. The thought of him not ever being here with me again had never even crossed my mind until that time. He was only 48 years old!

But God is good, and we have been blessed. Jerry recovered fairly well and after only six weeks, returned to work and has been working ever since. He is the dearest person in my life, and I can not imagine him not being by my side.

We have, through these many years, had award-winning battles with each other (which has made life nothing if not interesting), and we may not always have been as kind or considerate to one another as we should or could have been. We've at times even acted quite unbecoming to one another, but always, always, we have loved each other deeply.

This man who works a very difficult job (most people would not last through the day on one of Jerry's routes - especially on one of the dire weather days mentioned earlier), comes home to a wife who has been chronically ill for 28 of the almost 38 years of marriage. I have Chronic Fatigue Immune Dysfunction (you know... the "made-up illness," or rather the "yuppie flu stuff" we've all heard of), and Fibromyalgia, Chronic Myofascial Pain Disorder, Asthma and Arthritis. Along with a few other maladies and health considerations. The CFS alone is an elusive and little understood illness that often can, and has been known to completely devastate it's sufferers.

It possesses a 'cycling process' by which a person may have a period of seemingly good - or well days, to then be stricken with overwhelming exhaustion and flu-like symptoms and pain that can put one down for days, weeks, and sometimes even months at a time. The FM can add to the mix it's own brand of exhaustion and pain which can be utterly debilitating. The CMPD creates enormously painful knots anywhere on the body which then "network" from one place to another by forming rope-like cords connecting to one another, creating whole sections of tremendous pain. Often physical therapy is used to help alleviate these painful knots by manipulation, kneading them to flatten them out and getting them to release the stored toxins they contain, thereby bringing some relief from the systems of pain they have created.

When Jerry walks in the door from his work, it's then he faces his real job... for he never knows whether he will face Cinderella or one of the Wicked Step Sisters on any given day, in light of the mood swings and level of pain that these illnesses cause for me. And he doesn't know whether I've been upright and mobile for the day or had to stay down on the heating pad in bed the live long day.
But after he puts in a regular work day, regardless of whether it's been a good or a bad one, he comes in and 'pitches in' with supper if I'm struggling, and helps or takes over clean up after the meal if I can't do it (and I can't much of the time unfortunately). He vacuums and dusts, picks up around here, does laundry, runs errands, does yard work, car maintenance, takes care of our furry four leggers, and just anything and everything that may need done that I can not do on any given day.

I can tell you that I'd have given almost anything to have been able to write the chapters of our book of life together differently. To be able to change how it's unfolded before us, and to ensure that Jerry is not the one that has to do the lions-share of the work load that is done in our shared little world, instead of my not being able to do my part.

It's been more than frustrating at times, to just have to watch and carry a spectator's part in this scenario and feel so useless.
But my husband has not complained. He just does what a man's gotta do. He stepped up to the plate despite his own health struggles, or work demands upon him, or any other excuse for not taking his vows to love, honor, and cherish seriously. He does these things and more. And he is there for anyone else who needs him also. I can not tell you how many times he's dropped everything to go help someone who just needs an extra hand. When it is within his power to help, he's there.

There is no one who could ever compare to this wonderful man who truly is the hero God has gifted me with.
Although his sons have followed in their father's footsteps in these regards, which makes them close seconds. I'm very gratified that our sons gleaned all the good things from their dad's example through the years, and very proud of them both.

And in a world of sappy, idiotic, action adventure dime-a-dozen wide-screen-so-called hero's that are paraded before us, I am not fooled one whit. I know what a real hero is. And Jerry stands above them all. He may not go swinging through life on tree limbs rescuing damsels in distress, or swashing some dastardly dudes buckle, but he certainly has rescued THIS distressed damsel often enough in these almost 38 years together, and my fervent prayer is that he will continue to leap tall buildings with a single bound, and out run speeding bullets and locomotives in my life for a very long time to come.

Next time you see a short little mustached mail man carrying a satchel full of letters, give him a big smile and thumbs up! He deserves it. A thousand times over.
And you just never know, you may even catch a glimpse of his red cape underneath that blue postal uniform he's wearing, if you just look a little closer.
He's my husband Jerry.

And...he's my hero!

Rock Talk

You can not converse with a rock.
No matter how articulate and animated in making
your point, it always falls upon cold hard silence.
Rocks can not answer nor respond in kind.
There is no two way thing going on, so why try?
Crying, pounding, screaming and such mean nothing
to the solid mass of gray incapable of hearing it.
The only thing a rock is good for is bolstering up
a sagging wall, or skimming across a pond on
a brilliant Fall day.

So, I will take my feelings, stuff them in a jar,
and leave the rock in place to do what good rocks do.
My rock busies itself with tasks important only to him,
like...cleaning the grill, watching TV,
or reading the paper...while I whine.

I have poured myself out
only to have that unmoveable object
move out of range and into the rock garden, and
away from all the distasteful blatherings
of honest feelings shared.

And there the rock sits.
Oblivious and 'care'-less.
After all,
It's a known fact...
you can not converse
with a rock.

The Last Try

She said, "I just want to move clear away from here."
I said, "Well, how do you think that makes me feel?"
She said, "Well I didn't mean for you to take it personally."
And I told her that there was no other way to take it.

I said, "That really makes me feel bad."
She said, "Why do you feel that way?"
I told her that I feel I have no family.
She said that she was "tired of hearing that."

I said, "I'd like more than just a quick phone call
every few weeks, with an 'I love you'
tacked on at the end of the
conversation for good measure."
She said, "Well I just won't say it anymore then."
I said, "I'd like a sister that I can do things with,
be close to, have fun with."
She said, "I have a life to live, and so do you."

I poured out my heart to her
so she'd know how I feel.
She hung up the phone angry and defensive,
as I quietly closed the door of my heart to her

...for the very last time.

The Sister God Gave Me

Today I planted chrysanthemums in my little corner of the
yard that I can sit and look out upon. Before putting them in
the ground I had to pull weeds that had overtaken the little
growing seedling trees that had been trying to gain some
strength all summer long, a smattering of rose moss and a
few nicotenia plants that were blooming. In the very most
pointed place of the little corner, stands the yucca with it's spikey
leaves and shoots where blossoms once were, now turned to seed
pods.

All the while that I pulled those weeds today, my mind
was centered on my dear and beloved friend Shirley.
My God-picked sister from Louisiana. Shirley has been in
the hospital now three weeks. And in the duration of
those three weeks has stayed fairly well incoherent and
unable to converse with me or much of anyone. She barely
knows her surroundings at all. She was put into ICU this
morning because they could not register a blood pressure
for her. She was supposed to have an endoscopy today
to find the source of bleeding she's endured, but first
needed to be stabilized.

My gardening attempt, despite the physical pain of the day, was an
attempt to do something in an entirely helpless situation and to keep
my mind occupied in the midst of it all. Here I am, over a thousand
miles away and totally unable to even speak to my dearest friend. It's
odd how things work out in life.
Thirteen years ago I was new to things like message boards and
support forums online. I'd never really ever heard of them, but find
one I did. It was a tiny obscure little thing run by a 'Pastor John' in
California, on senac.com forums. It's where Shirley and I first met.

We were both scared to give out too much information about ourselves on the "Big Bad Internet," and took our time writing one another and getting to know what each of us was about.

In time, we became deep personal friends. There was hardly a day go by that we didn't talk on the phone, share our joys and frustrations, our aches and pains (having much the same illnesses). We've laughed together, cried together, and become all around best buddies. Ours is truly a sisters relationship in life. She and I have a spiritual bond which is understandable, since she has been convinced from the start that God brought us together. She has sisters (as well as brothers) that she is not able to be very close to in life. And sometimes, God will create family where there is no real sense of one. Such is the case for Shirley and myself.

As I bent to pull each weed I kept saying, "This is for you, Shirl." I thought of the 'weeds' that had crowded into her life over the last few years trying to choke out her vibrance, color and fragrance in life. Every time a deep rooted weed had it's ugly tendrils wrapped around her, she set about whacking it away one day at a time until it was effectively gone. And all the while she would let that wonderful bloom of hers shine forth in her little garden for everyone to see. How could anyone not be blessed by witnessing this brightly blooming flower amongst such a powerful weed bed?
And on I pulled.

These weeds I was working on pulled relatively easily, unlike the major monstrous ones she faced with her health. But all I could think of was that, here was a little corner that I was going to brighten the best that I could, just like shirley had done for so many around her.

How she would enjoy sitting out with her "critters," watching and laughing at the antics of "Petey and the rest of the gang" which consists of chipmunks, squirrels, and the multitude of birds that inhabit the back yard of Shirley and her dear hubby Joe. She and I would share our critter tales often from day to day.

I know Shirley would love the flowers in all their glory, that I was planting on her behalf today. And I will love seeing them spread out and brighten their little corner with the rusts, yellows, magentas and golds that will pop and be magnified with the autumn's sunny days ahead. And I can hardly wait to be able to tell her that she has a special place of prominence in the little corner of our tiny back yard that has flowers planted in her honor alone.
I'll come back out when they've grown and multiplied into brilliant bushes of glorious color and fragrant blooms to take pictures of Shirley's little flower garden, just so I can e-mail them to her when she's feeling better.

And each day I look out and see them or catch a whiff of their distinct fragrance, I will definitely think of Shirl. And until we can talk again and share and catch up on the bits and pieces of life's goings on together, they will be my reminder of her importance in my life, and the lives of all who know her.

She is the flower that grew out of the rock.
The one that stands out above the rest. The eye-catcher in a world of all the same kind in the flower bed.
She is the sister that God gave me. And today, she's the little corner of beautiful color in my flower garden.

When Sadie Sang The Blues

Slowly...she walked into the smoke fillied room,
like a wide awake dream.
She used to know this place.
Joe sat in the corner booth and chewed the fat with
the locals.

She was in there...deep in there.
Yet no one recognized her, for she'd changed.
But then, as the sax began wailing that familiar tune,
that young flaxen haired beauty that lived somewhere in the
corridors of that time riddled frame stepped up,
and left that old tired self behind.

There she was, this slip of a thing
slipped back into time.
Emerging from pitch black into light that fairly pumped
pure oxygen and electricity into the dark and dismal air
swirling around her head. The body in motion
began to sway.

And she lifted her hands and the soul came up.
That youth that she had always had inside, began that heart
pounding rhythm that propelled her feet. Up she floated and
pranced and danced until all heads spun. Until she'd lived life to
it's fullest, right there in that very moment, that very hour, that
very night.

She was the chord that struck eternity. She became the music.
She poured her heart out in the strange rainbow hues ablend with
stale liquor and thick madness. Until a gentle tap on her shoulder
reminded her of this continuum of time and space.

Gently the music and words began fading into the background. She took one long last draw of the cancer stick, and one final longing look at 'what used to be.' She slowly arose and unswervingly headed for the way out of the past.

She made a motion to the guys in the band.
She blew a kiss to Joe who bellowed out, "See ya next time old girl," and then...she was gone.
That golden moment etched for all time in their hearts. They just knew they'd been touched with a few moments of greatness... because Sadie sang the blues.

●

This is Ms. Shirley Braud's poem. I wrote it for her in or around 02' I think. We met online and she and I became the closest of friends. It took us awhile to get there though, as we'd first met back in the late 90's at a CFIDS support message board run by a 'Pastor John' out of California. Neither of us really knew what we were doing back then and we were uber-cautious of our privacy. But upon corresponding for quite awhile, we exchanged phone numbers and before you knew it, we were chatting almost daily. I live in Iowa, she in Louisiana. She is the subject of more than one of my writing endeavors. I just love the stuffin' out of this woman who easily could be my sister. And in fact, she is indeed the sister that God gave me. 'When Sadie Sang The Blues,' stems from Shirl's singing background. She used to sing with a band who traveled around Louisiana and beyond. She is an accomplished musician and still arranges music when she's able to. Ms. Shirl has chronic illness and even though she battles it daily in depth, she manages to keep those who know and love her laughing with her silliness and upbeat attitude. I am so privileged and blessed to know her. To call her sister/friend. She has gotten me through more rough spots in life than I can count. I can honestly say that I have never been closer to any one other person in my life than Shirley Braud. She indeed has been a heaven sent angel in my life.

Easter Memories

Easter is far and away my very favorite time of the year. Not only is it the promise of new life and a reminder of a love that overwhelms the senses of most, but it is when I seem to remember things long past in my life the most. I have some memories from way back that seem precious and few, but mine to keep tucked away in my heart just the same.

I pull them out every once in awhile just for the smile that they bring to my heart. Back when mom had "well days" and was able to do things. Joyful things that not only helped her to have a positive outlook on life, but everyone around her as well. And she spread her particular joy in many ways.

I had published a story about mom and the Easter Bonnets she made. And she would always, always take us shopping for just the right new frilly Easter outfits. From head to toe, I was always decked out in yellow or pink chiffon and crinolines replete with bows and of course brand new patent leather shoes and matching purse, and topping it all off, the Easter hat or flowers in my hair. A sight to behold. I felt special for all of mom's efforts. Easter sparks feelings in me of anticipation and hope. Maybe because it was at those times that I really felt like I belonged, like I mattered. And soon after Easter, there were other things to anticipate. Mom did many other things in very special ways as well. Not just at Easter.

May baskets were soon to follow. And oh, how people loved to receive mom's may baskets! And who could blame them? She (and I) would spend hours picking out the little paper cups, not too big, not too small. And sometimes she would wash up little food containers because they were "just the right size" to make a very special one for a particular someone special.

We would buy crepe paper rolls, the two-toned variety that you don't see anymore, pipe cleaners and glue. All the essential things for may basket making. It was truly an art, and my mom was the greatest may basket artiste' in the world (as far as I was concerned).

She possessed such a creative ability in so many areas, that I would loved to have had her around my whole life just to show me all the things she knew. Well, we would cut the proper lengths of ruffled crepe to fit around whatever container we'd end up using and either glue or staple it in layers, then we would thread another strip through long pipe cleaners and twist it around and around before attaching it to the sides of the container. Each piece was meticulously placed and twisted and shaped and adorned with ribbons, flowers, or paper curls, until a beautiful finished basket was ready to fill.

The filling was always fun because of course we got to eat some of the popcorn filling that always went in first, and sample the various candies and m&m's that were placed loosely inside. There was often a bow or a flower to add the last bit of flare, and many times there would be no candy at all. Just a basket full of fresh spring violets, bachelor buttons, daffodils and pansies. They were all beautiful. And then off we'd go, loading them in small flat boxes to distribute to unsuspecting friends and loved ones.

I was the one who got to jump out and run up to the door and knock or ring the bell and then scurry off, so as not to be seen. What fun that was!! I remember that dad drove us which seemed his contribution to the day's activities.

Yes, I do remember those days. They are but a mist from my past that seem as though they never really happened. But thankfully, I know that they did. And although there aren't many of them, I cherish each one that occasionally springs to mind at this time of year. And I can once again seem to relive and experience those happy days all over again.

Making memories with mom was something I didn't get to do much of. She was sick more than she was well in life. And the times she was well enough to be out, she and dad kept busy. She was the piano player in the band that was gone most week ends. I went along and slept on top of the coats piled high on the extra chairs and their chair trolleys at the Ogden City Hall Dances.

And as time passed and I grew a bit older, I occasionally stayed home on my own or with a friend. But the special 'memory making days with mom' so very vivid to me, were important to me then, and even some 50 odd years later still today.

So never underestimate the memories you make with a child. Your own or someone else's. It may well just be enough to last a lifetime and get them through the days where good memories become less and less.

You will never know the impact upon a child's heart from the good you do. Never let an opportunity pass to become that vital cherished moment in time in a little person's recollection.

These little moments have lasted sixty years in this old child's heart, and brought me comfort on a dreary enough day. They are part of my Easter Blessings and the Easter Memories kept within my heart.

Dedicated to Vida Marie Pharaoh - mom

•

When Mama Reads To Me

I'm glad our minds can do wondrous things. Like, store away
snippets of time from warm moments spent, then turn them into
cherished memories.
And keep on file beautiful sights and sounds and voices.
Sometimes, when I have trouble sleeping at night, I get up and
grab a good book, or...THE Good Book, and begin reading with
my mind's recollection of mama's voice. And before I know it,
she's reading to me. And the words mean so much more.
They are alive and I can concentrate on what they're really saying
to my heart.
As the years have passed, the memory of mama's voice is
sometimes harder to recall...but I still try. Even mama's
reprimand now, would be sweet lyrical music to my soul,
if I could only hear it.
So I practice listening for her voice often, just as you can
with all those you have loved in life gone on before you.
I know God exists. I know it each time I pick up a book and
mama reads to me.

•

Especially for Chad and Jason.
Life is uncertain at best, and things can change
in the blink of an eye. If you should awaken tomorrow
to find me gone, read with my voice in your heart.
I will always be with you in life.
I will always love you. And my love can
read you through
the pages of life and greet you,
the first morning of
eternity.
Love, mama

The Jerry Chair

Easin' on into the land
where time has no constraint.
And there's no need for clocks and schedules
and ne'ry a complaint.

When entire days can be spent afishin'
if a fella has a mind to go.
And words like 'hurry' and 'hey, we're late'
have no meanin', don'tcha know?

They say retirin' is just grand,
and we know it must be so.
To be able to see the things you want
and go where you wanna' go.

We hope this newfound freedom,
gained as you retire,
will save this poor ole' rockin' chair
from becomin' kindlin' fire.

The two of you will have a ball
rockin' away the extra hours now free'd.
And it won't mind a little bit
if you slow down and adjust it's speed.

So by all means, familiarize
your tail end with this chair.
Cause now that you're a man of leisure,
you've got the time to spare!

(given to my brother Jerry, June 28, 2003 with a painted black
rocking chair with his name prominently displayed upon a brass
name plate attached to the back and a big bow, for his retirement)

The Twelve Days of Ornish

(written for cohort 4 at the Iowa Heart Center's Dr. Dean Ornish
Heart Reversal Trial in DesMoines, of which Jerry and I were a part)

On the FIRST day of Ornish, Tom Lowe said to me
You're as Flabby as you can be. (Lloyd)

On the 2ND day of Ornish, Mandy said to me,
No more eating bad stuff. (Renee)

On the 3RD day of Ornish, Dr. Wick, he said to me,
Ya gotta change your life. (Gary)

On the 4TH day of Ornish, Victoria said to me,
This program's not for wimps. (Norma)

On the 5TH day of Ornish, Don Gilbert said to me,
HOW DO YOU FEEL? (Lin)

On the 6TH day of Ornish, Diane said to me,
No more eating chocolate. (Joan)

On the 7TH day of Ornish, Carol said to me,
Are we having fun yet? (Shelby)

On the 8TH day of Ornish, Troy Bond said to me,
Now go VISUALIZE yourself a TREE!
(after the first time sung, sing repetitive verse with only VISUALIZE
and TREE) (Tom)

On the 9TH day of Ornish, Terrisue said unto me,
You can work things out. (Connie)

57

On the 10TH day of Ornish, my true love said to me,
What have we gotten into? (Jerry)

On the 11TH day of Ornish, Michelle said to me,
You're all a bunch of whiners. (Judy)

On the 12TH day of Ornish, the whole group said to me,
Where'd ya put the Bean-O? (Jim)

VERY LAST VERSE:
On the last day of Ornish, these dear friends said to me,
We've all done really good...
On that we surely do agree! (Everyone)

(sung to the tune of the Twelve Days of Christmas}
I included this because it was quite a memory and an experience for
Jerry and I. We made good friends in that program and it actually
turned out to be a very beneficial and rewarding time for us
traveling to DesMoines three days a week. The dedication and
camaraderie of the group, and those professionals who were
determined to help us all, was a blessing we would never forget.

•

Poet

I'm a poet, and I know it.
Though my words oft' times won't show it.
And my verse can be terse,
when at times I converse.
Tis true, so true, tis' sad but true.
Can't help but rhyme,
what shall I do?
Plant word seed and grow it.
And hope beyond hope
foul frequent brainstorms
won't blow it!

The Downhill Side Of Fifty

Time has dulled the senses, I can't see too good no more.
On the down hill side of fifty, might as well be one
hundred and four!
My grin greets me each mornin,' as I squint to see myself. Don't need
to look in a mirror no more, I keep my smile in a jar on the shelf.
Yep, these bones won't do no disco now, got to buy some liniment.
Now that I'm in my fifties, lands...
I wonder where time went?! I move a little slower now, can't rock n'
roll or jump no pews.
The middle aged spread has done spread out! Got the "downhill
fifty" blues.
And that ole' (Joyce) never looked so cute, I'd like
to show her a thing or two. But on the downhill side of fifty, just
can't remember what to do!
Yep! Those metallic years have crept up fast. Don't do no good to
pine.
But as long as I've got my rockin' chair,
I know that I'll do
fine.
I'll sit and spit and gum some candy, and think of by gone days.
When the down hill side of fifty, to me was just a phrase. Now I'll go
and join the 'old folks' as they sit around the fire.
Cause' on the downhill side of fifty friend,
you might as well retire!

•

Read to Chris O. on her 30th birthday (instead of 50th as originally written)
at Lanny and Barb Stumbo's, and brother Jerry on his 50th birthday
celebration December 8th, 1987. The only difference was that I substituted
Chris's hubby's name, Rodger for Joyce and the 20th stanza read, "I'll sit
and knit" instead of "sit and spit." I remember that Chris was not a bit
happy at turning 30. She was the last of our group to do so. And we set
about finding as many crazy things to make the transition as pleasant and
almost painless as possible. I had taken pains in my search and found an
ancient lace up corset from the dark ages, and ugly black orthopedic shoes,
a black shawl, wig and old bifocals, and our dentist back then even gave me
a pair of "uppers" to wrap up for her. All in all, I don't think she ever
forgot...or forgave, us!

Tricky Dick Ticks

Twas' the nite before surgery when throughout the corridor,
a nervous hush settled in as we all paced the floor.
The doctors and nurses were poised for the fight.
We all buckled down for a long summer's night.
The seconds and minutes ticked by the hour,
as we hoped and prayed trusting our higher power.

Knowing our Dick would soon be out of our care,
we trusted the Lord and the good staff that was there.
We waited and hoped and waited some more.
Watching for good news to walk through the door.
The nurses were good to keep us updated,
to help keep our hopes from becoming deflated.
Time wore us down, the clock was defeating.
Then came the good news...Dick's new heart was beating!

We all gave a whoop and started to cheer,
we knew in a flash there was no need to fear.
And who knew we'd get to celebrate in a year,
Dick's being alive, that's the reason we're here.
To tell you we love you and you're well on your way,
so the next 100 years we can now truly say;
Happy Father's Day All, and to all a good day!!
•
There once was a fella named Dick
Whose ticker did not want to tick.
So we got him a new one,
A tried and true blue one,
Now tricky Dick won't be sick!

(Written for the 1st year anniversary of Dick's heart transplant in
DesMoines, Iowa, Father's Day June 1989. And I'm very happy to say
that this year 2009, allowed us our 20th year of celebration with Dick
and family.) We owe our heartfelt gratitude to the young man and his
family that made this possible for us. God bless them.

The Preacher Perfect

Some people say the preacher
speaks a little too loud!
Others may moan and mumble,
"Why can't he speak up in a crowd?"
Why, every time I phone him,
he's never there at all.
He's supposed to stay at home
and be at our beck and call!
Some say he never visits, or
his visits are scarce at best.
While others lament, "he's just nosey,"
"He should give the visiting a rest."
Some say they heard him comment on
Mrs. Jones' hat.
"Why, he wouldn't give me the time of day,
what do ya make of that?"
He eats too much at pot lucks,
"He wouldn't eat my stew!"
Some say he tries to please too much,
what's a discerning man to do?
Yep, the preacher just bout' hears it all.
Everything from bad to good.
But may we all remember that
he's just doin' what he should.
So pastor if you're ever
in the midst of critical frustration,
remember you can't please folks all the time
in every situation.
And as far as pleasin' someone,
it's pleasin' God that's best.
If you've satisfied one hungry heart,
the Lord will please the rest.
February 25, 1991

Life is Fickle

Fickle life how it teases.
Filling minds with what ere' it
pleases.
A day is born and with it's light,
seconds flee, taking wings in
flight.
We who dwell upon the earth
die in minutes from our
very birth.
Live well each moment
that comes to you.
Good life, it's blessings
are far too few.
Yes fickle life
will have
it's due.

The Thief

There's nothing more keenly abjectly sublime,
than the occasional glance backward to ponder
the essence of time.
And time holds value second to none.
For the memories therein
and all the good things been done.
So savor time captured, as 'mind-pictures' so real.
For quickly time leaps
those glad memories to steal.

Dear John With A Twist

Dear John,

Before you leave, I must thank you for the good times we must have had. I really didn't care for you, but you thought I had it bad. Of course, I let on that I cared, it was the only thing to do. But, it was an absurdity to think that I could ever really love you.

You tried every trick there was to make me fall for you, but I only laughed because before we started, I knew we'd be through.I played your game just like a pro, I fooled you all the way. The intent I had was just a joke and I scoffed at the idea of our "wedding day."

You know, it sure is funny though, how you seemed to dominate me. But I didn't care, and I didn't know that's how you'd planned it to be. Sure, you thought you had me wrapped up tight, and when I gave all that I could...what you felt for me was slight, and I took more than anyone should.

But don't let these words throw you by the little things that I've just said. I guess I've led you on now, about as far as I could have led. You see, this pain in my heart isn't real. I'm just kidding you (and myself). The bargain we made was just a bad deal, and now I'll climb back up on my shelf. I'll pick myself up, dust myself off, and convince you I didn't fall. For these tears are only make believe...I've never loved you at all.

(every teenager experiences a broken heart at some point. I wrote this in 1966 , but couldn't tell you if you paid me, who I wrote it about back then. Ahhh, the angst and passions of the mixed up teenaged girl/or guy)

Night Cry

Well I've been there, and it's lonely and hard
like a piece of stone.
And you stand there in the quiet and look out
at things unknown.
And the cool wind whispers soft
upon your face.
As you struggle, seeking blindly,
looking outward to find your place.
But the longing and the aching
just keep on until they've run you
in the ground.
And you shout out such a cry
and it's silent,
because you've never really made a sound.
Oh, how do you know where to go
if you've never been there before?
And it's tough,
so wise up fast and try to find out
the score.
And it's rough, you know I've been
there and it's hard like a piece of
stone.
And you just stand there in the quiet
and you see that you're really
all alone.

(Life as a young teen for me was difficult. And as you can see
in this writing from back then, filled with the emotional struggles
that seemed to go along with the difficulties. Sometimes a person
can be affected profoundly for life by the loneliness and isolation
felt as a kid. I carry that imprint upon my sixty year old heart as
proof).

Roving 'Bed'lam

Ms. Grishom's (published on mindmills/perspectives) rocking chair mystery prompted memories of my own youthful curious events. Many having to do with my Grandma Pharaoh's 'haunted' farm! She lived in Nebraska with my Uncle Jim, a kind and gentle man whom I loved dearly.

On one particular visit, grandma had sent me into the middle bedroom to look for a treasure to take home from within the many boxes stored there. I never left grandma's empty handed.
As I leaned with my back up against grandma's big old iron bed, (actually it was the 'company bed' from the extra room, not the one that grandma slept in) waiting for her to come in and help me find my prize, the big old iron bed moved.

Now I was a wee little thing, and smart enough to know or at least realize, that I wasn't strong enough to be the one that moved the bed. Well, I shot out of there and ran to grandma's side in a panic, shouting to her and uncle Jim and my parents that the bed had moved all by itself! Well, unnerving as all that was to a small kid, it was sort of just smoothed over by all the grown ups at the time, and grandma eventually took my hand and led the way back into "that spooky room" to retrieve my little keepsake from the visit.

I hadn't given it much thought until years later when my husband & I had taken our then two small boys to visit Uncle Jim and stayed overnight. I recounted the incident about the haunted bed to Uncle Jim the next day to see if he remembered it. He got this big grin on his face and chuckled that I had just slept in that bed! So much for the spooky memory!

It was only after all this that I discovered that my sisters (both a bit older than myself), had experienced even more bizarre incidents concerning that old bed.

It seems that at different times when they were little, they had each stayed overnight at grandma's in that bed. And each of them on those separate occasions, had experienced the end of that big old heavy iron bed raising up at least a foot off of the floor (with them still in it), terrifying them half to death! Or - such is their recollection of these frightening childhood bugaboos.

They both relate that they too ran screaming out to be rescued from the terror of this restless bed directly to Uncle Jim, who being the wonderful rescuer of little girls, proceeded to go in and promptly inspect the suspicious bed. The covers, the floor, and anything else suspected of causing such a phenomenon! Of course he never found a thing, but to this day that bed is still a family legend. We still get goose bumps, and all those scary feelings come flooding back at the mere mention of grandma's old iron bed!

There were many other strange things that had happened way back then at grandma's farm. Things that make one wonder if things really do go 'Bump in the night', or if they're to remain just the wild imaginings of active youthful minds.

But one thing I do know, to this day I have this odd compelling attraction toward old iron beds that I may happen upon in quaint antique shops here and there. Maybe they just remind me of the farm and grandma, or quite possibly one of the sweetest, nicest, kindest uncles in the world. Uncle Jim, you were the greatest and I miss you...iron bed and all.

JAMES CURTIS PHARAOH SERVED IN WWII. HE HUNTED ARROWHEADS ON THEIR FARM FOR YEARS, ACCUMULATING ONE OF THE LARGEST COLLECTIONS EVER FOUND IN THE AREA. HE WOULD TAKE THEM INTO GRADE SCHOOLS TO SHOW QUITE OFTEN. HE DONATED THE BULK OF HIS COLLECTION TO A LOCAL MUSEUM. HE WAS A KIND AND WONDERFUL MAN WHO, AFTER SERVING HIS COUNTRY, CAME BACK AND TOOK CARE OF MY GRANDMA UNTIL HER DEATH. HE REMAINED IN HIS HOME TOWN ALL OF HIS LIFE, A LOVING LOYAL FRIEND TO THE ENTIRE COMMUNITY OF PERU, NEBRASKA. AND IS SOMEONE I'LL NEVER FORGET.

Fairy Tale

Thoughts scattered as Dandelion tufts
in the winds of a warm Spring day.
Time has sifted the ages and settled
into lines and grooves that marked
the paths traveled upon a once fresh,
smooth, silken face.
So many unanswered questions,
now set adrift upon a dark troubled sea.
Out of time, Out of space
Out of purpose...out of place.

The chant drolls on in endless droning
that only her ears hear. And dull life
is all too real to one who began a fairy princess.
And there are no kingdoms
left to reign in, no subjects loyal and true.
And glass slippers are broken,
and handsome rescuer's no longer
pass her way.
Where ever did time scamper?
That good life lived...so far gone.
Only vague memories of a woman
no one really ever saw in life,
slipped away from earth in a sigh.
Out of time, Out of space
Out of purpose...out of place.

Love Tangled

Tripped into a void.
Fallen into a tumble.
Eyes opened wide.
Now the heart's
in a jumble.

Endless the fall.

Forever I Will Love You

Two young teenyboppers just starting out in life. He said, "You know I love you so...would you consent to be my wife?"
She answered very quickly, with a twinkle in her eye,
And made that young man jump for joy when he heard "Yes" as her reply.
The years, they've passed so swiftly. So many cherished moments to recall. And step by step and side by side, they've been together in them all. She asked, "Will you still love me...when we've both turned old and gray?" He looked deep into her eyes and said, "Just try to keep me away."
"I've loved you from the beginning, right from the very start."
She smiled and held him oh, so close...she could feel every beat of his heart.
And hand in hand they walked the pathways, God chose especially for the two, and blessings came as well as storms, that had to be weathered through.
And still today that love does shine, as strong as ever it had before,
And now when she asks, "Do you love me still?" She hears, "I could not love you more."
So time and all life's circumstance can not dim this love so true.
When in another ninety years we'll hear them say,"My dear, I will always, always, always and forever...and forever always, love you."

For Jerry and Joyce on the occasion of their
49th wedding anniversary, November 3rd, 2008...with love.

My beloved sister-in-law left us just four days shy of her 50th Golden Wedding anniversary with her Jerry, October 30th this year, 2009. She was and still is, so loved by her entire family and missed every day. I was fortunate to be able to share this poem with her via a special web page I'd made for them just the year before. God allowed this small blessing, for which I will always be grateful. For I could not possibly have ever known then, that she would not be here to read it for their fiftieth year together.

68

The Burn

I have felt it all.
The warm breaths whispered against
anticipation's quivering gates,
awaiting entrance into depths
not dared imagined.
The singe of passions laid bare and openly taunted.
Beckoning to be pacified over and over again.

Caresses, tender in the night, that are born
of fibers woven gently around the heart,
attached firmly to the soul,
that are one and the same.
The rush of air that enters as one inhales pleasure
born sweetly from within the chambers
of love's
dwelling places.

Then exhaled as pure sustenance of life itself.
There are no words of description.
Breathe in...breathe out,
Count each heartbeat slowly
and drink in the moment,
while it is the moment captured.

For love too often is a memory.
Like a faded rose removed from the Prom's
pink chiffon.
Long gone, but not forgotten.
And those feelings can ride away forever
towards a sun that never sets,
In a heart that always thirsts.

Dedicated to the one who "Doesn't believe love exists." Truly
it does. And if you find it, you'll move heaven and earth to
hold on to it. Even when it pales with time, it is worth every
minute you've ever lived it.

The Note

(written for the anonymous round of
poetry at 'mirable visu '- an online writing group)

It couldn't be disregarded.
Laying there for days. As if
ignoring it would make it vanish.
Or at the very least, quell the impulses
evoked by it's somber phrasing.
Words hastily scrawled by one no longer
present to offend. Leaping off the paper and
straight into her soul.
Standing at the window reflecting upon better days,
she's drawn back to the table where dust has begun
to settle all around it.
Strange, how such a small scrap of paper and words
coarsely written can alter one's world so utterly.
The closet, now empty.
The blinds, drawn shut and the house sealed.
The silence deafening, as every nook and cranny
fills with sorrow.
She picks up the slip of paper with hands all a tremble.
And reads the note for the last time.
Those four words summing up twenty-eight years of
loving sacrifice and great effort, of wonderful endearing
memories, of lives lived happily...but not ever after.
Tucking it away into the pages of her Bible,
her heart is etched and forever scarred
with the message held within...
"Today, I'm leaving you."

Some Hearts Broken

Some broken hearts can be patched
pieced and tied, enough to continue beating on.
They may quiver and shake and rumble and whimper,
yet manage to do the work set before them.
Some hearts carry enormous struggle to the point
that all of life is squeezed and oozing out.
But that flattened, feeble, faintly beating heart
does not stay down. No,
it picks itself up and shifts the load and carries on.
Hearts so small can almost burst from joys and
laughter at the good in life.
And still they calm to catch the tears that flow
from the pain that comes to those they love,
to offer strength and offer hope.
To live is to feel.
To feel is life. And at the center of life,
the hub of all things...lies the heart.
With rhythmic precision keeping time with all
that makes life so real.
In so doing, we become real. We are the rhythm,
the pulse that spins the world.
And perhaps we are those who in the long journey,
will keep up with the beat.
When these weak vessels which hold so much of life
that it seems they will break, encounter love,
encounter hate, and learn from them that the realm of both
always contains

Some hearts broken.

Captured

It was a hot and steamy night.
White sands were cool and the waters
washed over her,
like a new beginning.

Desire was her name, and she came to play a game.

Because of the pain he'd caused.
Because it was time for her to forget.
But she hadn't expected...this.
The gentle brush of a stranger's eyes
that caressed a yearning soul,
that felt like hope
all over again.
That felt...
like a first kiss.

And who was this lingering question
that had caught her unaware?
And why had she been chosen?
The balmy summer night's breeze
kept whispering..."This is him...this
is him."

But would the heart that held such sorrow
be willing to become undone once more?
Could she allow him in?
Or would she just
keep walking?

Wanting was her name, and she came to play a game.

One touch told it all.
That one embrace wiped away all the sadness
and reserve.
And the two drew closer.

Their warm breath's upon each others cheeks.
The dark and dancing eyes that kept inviting more.
The hearts met, the souls connected
with a cord that she knew would bind them at once
and forever.

He had captured her.

And it's been said that on certain quiet nights,
on the southern most tip of the lovely island shores,
one can see the shadowed figures of two lovers dancing
against moonlit backdrop and star sparkled skies.
Gazing only at one another, unaware of the world.
Caught up in a passion like none other
has ever felt before.

From loves long burned into cold and useless ash,
arose a mighty raging, furious and all consuming
fire of the souls.

Ecstasy was her name, and she knew this was no game.

For his love alone could fan the flame
to fuel the fire of her broken heart.
To restore love's hope.
To wipe away the pain
and bring life to her again.
- 2002 -

Heart of Stone

I have fallen oh so far away, from where first we'd met.
Living large and on my own, on streets washed with regret. I do
remember sunlight. But with each day the memory fades of the ever
elusive light. The warm evasive spark of life that used to exist in You.

And it wasn't you who walked away. I'm the one to blame.
Yours was the only radiant color in a sea of black and gray.
Yours the technicolor hope in random 'all the same'.

I am lost, so very lost...I can't remember which way's home.
Doomed now to just exist, not live, and trek this way alone.
The time is come, I stand on trial before the judge of all mankind.
The verdict, "Life!"

Endless, gut-wrenching, excruciating life with no hope.
Hope, never to be found again. You are LIFE! You are Truth! And the
hope this mortal coil rejected and cast aside so carelessly without a
second thought. Now it seems I'll be lost forever. Yet I know you're
out there waiting. And I here...too ashamed to approach, and
uncertain how to even start.

For the poisonous arrow of betrayal fashioned with my own two
hands, has turned and pierced your heart. How can I ask forgiveness?
When sin's death grip upon me lies? And the soul within my bosom,
as a whimpering pup cries. I am no more able now, to walk the path
you trod. The only path directed toward the very throne of God.

I had everything, wondrous gifts all...and didn't even know. Until
they, as dried crumbling leaves silently fell away to be trampled into
dust beneath these burdensome feet. All the while I knew what I was
doing, and yet...the feet kept walking. Until now....arrived at this
place I do not recognize at all. Fading apparitions remain. Shadows of
what could have been, had I just not held on to...this heart of stone.

Taking Stock

After the angst, what's to blame
for all the mucking up we do
in life?
You can't lay claim to that,
once you're thirty-five.
Get up and out
lazy, good-for-nothing, no good
drudge of a life!
If that's what you can call it.
Probably it's more a mere
imitation of
what life's supposed to be
but fallen short.
Who knows such things?
And would anyone care,
even if they did?
I'm hapless to escape.
There are no longer any
routes out of the city,
and everyone needs a
good escape route.
A good long swim
at the bottom
of the ocean might
suffice, or...A very
forgiving
God.

That's What You Think

You think you're great...and you are.
You're charming, eloquent and devout.
You think you make the world turn.
You think these things.
You've got a lot going for yourself, you
surely do, you can tell.
You can turn on, turn off, pick up, or shut down
anyone at anytime.
Go on and laugh at the unfortunates, they all deserve it
you know. Because they can't do the things you can do, or
don't have the things that you have.
Don't ever tie yourself down to anyone
or you may end up liking them too overly much and then
your social life would be gone.
You think you owe nothing to no one, and you don't.
You have feelings, we can tell.
You show them at all the most inappropriate times.
You can't possibly hurt anyone by leading them on, you
don't do that sort of thing. And your friends are all so valued
that you'd never underhand them or talk behind their backs.
You're delightful, pleasant, and do little wrong.
At least, not enough to show. Being nice just comes naturally
to you.
You think these things, you think these things.
Yes, honestly you do.
But you really must take a better look at yourself,
a mirror shows two sides of you.

- 1966 -

Glimmerlax

Stepping out to Glimmerlax where all that glitters gleams.
And fiery golden starlight dwells amidst flowing silver
streams.

And butterflies do flutter by upon their busy rounds.
And listening in the quiet tide nets a score of blended sound.
But proceed with caution, look carefully. Trust not first sound
nor sight.
For beneath the layer of fairy dust lies darkness void of light.

In this fantasy land of glitz and glimmer, that hold all the
dreams little eyes can behold, one may well be granted all,
and yet be left barren, lonely and cold.
For all that glitters is not what it seems, or so it is foretold.

It beckons and pulls you merrily, anxious to take your hand.
To then walk you through the revelry to a strange and
frightening land.
Once you've tasted and indulged, all your carnal pleasures
filled, it drags you down it's alleyways dark,
of sorrows and ill will.

And the beauty and flash, clamor, glamour and fun,
is now replaced with the knowledge of what's been done.

And you'll turn to run away, escape...hide your eyes in shame.
And the bejeweled pathway's now grown thick with weeds
will make you stumble on in pain.

For now there is no turning back, in dis-ease you'll forever
roam, and long for days of no regret
before Glimmerlax became your home.

Daddy's Arms

The illness took it's toll.
It lasted several years.
Brought dangers, suffering,
struggles, but most of all...tears.

How sick must one become?
How long the conflict be?
Before relief and sweet release
and healing come to me?
I did exactly what I should.
Although pride held me tight.
The step of faith was all He asked,
my Savior fought the fight.

Yes, sin's sickness pummeled me
through years of grief and pain.
What set out to maim and to destroy
was used for heaven's gain.
When one struggles for so long
with the illness from sin's harms,
a blessed death results
in a daddy's waiting arms.

Death to self and sin.
No longer battling life.
For my life ended just this night,
and so ended all my strife.
I crossed over not alone,
sailed death's sea without alarms.
For the dying of self to sin took place,
in my daddy's loving arms.

In Search of Life

It's a fine line betwixt life real and life imagined. When we go to
places we've never been and eagerly seek out the familiar, or
those things which evoke excitement in the discovery of our
common bonds with what's been..
We search behind rough concrete and stone for glimpses
of lives once lived there. We touch cold walls, running
our hands lightly over hard uneven bricks built upon the bones of
centuries past.
Our minds query, "What manner of people lived here?"
"What stories would these walls have to tell?"
Did they enfold laughter and brightness, or dark treachery
and deceit? Did love dwell here? Or was there encased within,
only cruelty, hatred, and bitterness?
Years come and go and stately ghosts are left behind as a visual
testament to what once had meaning.
But who could really know their meaning now? We hunger for
antiquities that say, "Your life was born of this...this was your
point of origin." Searching for meaning through decades of stone
and glass, in pieces of what's past.
More than walls and relics and tangible things,
love seeded within the hearts of those left behind by those long
traveled on, are the foundations and building blocks from which
life is constructed one generation to the next.
Like a strong invisible cord that secretly ties it all together from
one life to another. From one soul to the collective souls of
mankind.
Our beginnings can not be found in bricks and mortared ruins
left in time, but rather the legacies of how one spends the love
given them to impart to others. The love that permanently
imprints the hearts and lives of those they've met on the way,
while searching for life.

Tailor of Life

Thread the needle one more time
a broken heart to mend.
There's a hole in this old life,
that needs darned once again.
Sew another twenty stitches
and hope that it will do.
Don't you know the Master Tailor
can make a new pattern
just for you?
Patch a place much worn with
heartache and care.
Restyle an old long lived life there.
Tuck in this memory, let out a few.
There's One who can sew it all up for you.
Jesus, Tailor of my life,
you've the perfect fit for me.
Cut and match each single piece
to be what you want it to be.
The beautiful finished design of life
You first saw in me.

For WMPF (Women's Missionary Prayer Fellowship) Banquet,
'Patterns For Living' - speaker, Mrs. Heckman (Dale's mom).
Read as "anonymous" by Leora Stumbo to the ladies. 4/28/80

As I Have Loved You

If I were you and loved by me, would I have the love Jesus meant it to
be? Would I feel restricted or ill at ease, like I must conform or
perform to please? Would I in trouble run quickly to share, or just run
away from you finding judgment there?

If I were you and loved by me, what kind of friend would I find
you to be? Quick to anger and to speak? Slow to understand or turn
the other cheek? How quickly I'd learn my deficiencies...if I were you,
and loved by me. 9/08/80 for Chris - (my self examination in
friendship).

But I'm Just A Worm Lord

Look at that! He's chewing up everything in sight!
Chomp, chomp, gobble, gobble...don't get in his way, whatever you
do!

But he's only doing what he knows he must to survive.

What's he doin' now? Wrapping himself up like that? Does he think
he can escape life in that thing?

He's probably giving himself time to reflect back on his life.

Look at that! I've never seen anything like it in my life!
Why's he fighting so? Kicking, punching, wearing himself into a
wreck, using every tiny ounce of energy he's got. There won't be
anything left of him!

He's only doing what comes naturally to him.

Wow! He broke through! What a change! Did you ever see anyone so
beautiful? Hey...he can fly! He must've had help. Nobody can change
and become a new creature on his own. Hey...are you listening to
me?

*Yes, my son...I'm listening. I've been there through the whole experience. I
was there when he knew nothing better than chomping up everything in
sight. I was with him in his little shelter, and in his terrible struggle to break
away from the old and into the new. Of course he fought with all he had, he
was afraid to change. Afraid the world would suck him in again and he'd go
back to chomping away with the rest of them. But I was there to help him
become something new and beautiful, and I'm still here. Tell me, why do you
squirm? Don't you know my love can create a beautiful butterfly
from any lowly little worm?*

dedicated to all who know the struggle of rebirth and the triumphant
end of those who live through it.

And Yet I Am Afflicted

Oh Lord, my eyes can see, but I am blind.
For I've seen the multitude of lost and hungry people
and passed them by.
Oh Lord, my ears can hear, but I am deaf.
For the mounting cries of babes, and the hungry and suffering
have eluded me.
My mouth can speak, yet I am dumb.
From out of it comes nothing as I see injustice rise above and
round about me, I do not cry out!
My limbs and feet are whole oh Lord, yet I am lame.
For I turned and walked, no...ran...from all that would involve
me in these troubled people's lives.
My hands can work, yet they are still.
As others reach out to grasp them, I pull away,
not wanting to touch this dirty throng.
My heart still beats, but I am dead.
Indifferent to the needs around me.
Yes, I've been given health, yet I am afflicted.
Sorely with a dread disease.
To do not your will for me oh Lord, but
as I may well please.
Oh heal me Lord, restore me.
Make me whole again, I pray.
That I may love and serve you through
someone else today.

(Given to Judy Heckman in 1979 because she asked if she could
have it. I always thought she might try to write a song from it..
She's very talented in that regard.)

Rest your weary bones, Jesus gives you perfect peace.
Bound with a tired soul? Jesus gives you sweet release.
There is no other comfort, no other place to be...
than found in Jesus' perfect grace,
His gift of love to you
and me.

Refrain

The player of the music
makes it look so graceful.
The bow gliding across the strings
slowly drifting, lifting, and singing
it's mournful song.
And it's a beauty that strikes the chords
circling around about me.
Comforting, touching,
where mere word and human gesture
fail. They could never enter in.
Then it dances through the corridors
of my heart to fast become
a part of me.
Oh, holy strains which echo
ere' so gently cross'd my soul,
How thankful to my God I am,
that He brought you to me.
And for ears to hear your calling
which stirs within my heart
an indescribable joy, with
inescapable assurance,
that You are always...

where I am.

Lord, if you make the music...
I'll forever be your song.

Upon This Rock

I too, am Petra.
I, the feminine counterpart, am quick to react then learn the lesson. The one unwilling to listen because that would be admitting my weakness. And upon listening, then finding the inner struggle too tremendous a force to reckon with just because of my mind's constant questioning. I would barrage Him with questions. After all, I am as Peter...a logical thinking, typically reactive personality. I respond to the awesomeness of God and He draws me closer.
Then I stomp my feet in anger when I can not make my thoughts line up with His. My very nature is 'Petra' to the core.
And yet God in His infinite and tender mercy through Jesus, found the very epicenter of my being and somehow overlooked my impetuosity and bullheaded ways to find the softness in my soul.

How He could ever find anything of worth in there is quite the puzzlement of my life. For stone-cold reactionaries and passionate thinkers do not change quickly, if at all.
Peter after all, cut off poor Malchus' ear if you remember. And then there was the denial...three times. Ah, that was it! The weakness that betrayed the tough exterior. The weakness that Christ could use for His greater glory. And He saw it all along.
Peter did not. No self-respecting Petra does. Until God's own light reveals it in His matchless ways.

And I remember Jesus' words, "Upon this rock, I will build my church." Yes, the tough and stony exterior needed to have it's weakness's exposed first. Because only then could the crumbling mortar be revealed and replaced lovingly with God's own hand-hewn stone.

The cracked unstable rock replaced by those of His own choosing by His hands alone, to withstand the gale forces and fury from the gates of hell.

I too, am 'Petra' Lord.
Remove the cracked, unstable, and flawed stones in my character, my ways, my life, that make my foundation shaky. I too, wish to hear you say, "Upon this rock...I will build."
9/20/94

•

There is a quiet inner strength that belies the outer shell sporting small cracks and imperfections in the crevices all about. Held together by strength unseen to the human eye. Showing wear and tear and yet... unyielding to every hammer's blow.
It is:
His hope in us.
  His strength.
   His...Petra.

•

Every day that we can progress an inch means that we will eventually make the mile.

•

I love "me" is often just as
important as the "I love you."

Desert Builder

Today you may feel like the smallest grain of sand in the Mojave.
Buried beneath the weight of tons above you.
Just can't seem to muster enough strength to work your way up and
out where a fair wind could blow you over into brighter worlds.
Like maybe, some ocean front property by a sea-sprayed beach,
where seagulls sport and small feet patter about making sand castles
and fun.

Or where perhaps wet shorelines would give you a chance to stick,
for a little while anyway. Until the next big wave takes you out to sea
to then be buried beneath the weight of tons above you. Where you
just can't seem to muster enough strength to work your way up and
out from under the ocean's deep, to where cool waters could sail you
into new adventuresome worlds.

But today, just try to remember...
God knows exactly where you are little sand grain.
We don't always end up in life where our sights were first set.
And we may well lose sight of ourselves somewhere in life's
whirl of circumstances that we've little control over, or in the
turbulent troubles and struggles that come.

We very well may become buried under weights
of unfulfilled dreams and promises unkept, broken hearts,
and deep longings that really mattered.
Yes, we may feel quite insignificant and often hopeless but, we
matter significantly in the greater scheme of things.

Especially to the One who created us for His greater purposes.
He built entire seascapes and deserts that began with but one...
tiny grain of sand.

An Easter Heart

I can not explain the peace of heart that is mine because of the resurrection of Jesus Christ. There just are no words for it.
But I can say in so many words, that the gratitude that I have from knowing that the trials of life which come, will end at some point in time, and the promise of a secure eternal life free of them is just AWESOME beyond belief!

In fact, I know that everything about the truth and the hope of the resurrection may seem to some, beyond belief.

But ask any dull and barely beating heart that has awakened to it's reality, and they will tell you that it is not only believable, but miraculous. It is a hope and joy that can never be shaken, no matter what perils of life may come.

Yes, trials and tribulations come. Everyone faces insurmountable odds at some point in life, others sooner than some. And if the only seemingly insurmountable odd you face up til' now is death, then be rest assured that even that has been overcome for you by one huge, overpowering, indescribable act of love like none other.

May that act of love, whether you believe it or not, or know it's full significance or not, or whether you even give it a second thought past a colored egg or a lily that blooms on your mantle, or no thought at all, become deeply significant to you somehow in your heart. And from one such renewed from a once dull and barely beating heart, to you and yours...may you be filled with the brilliant hope and promise of real life without end, real joy that will carry you through hardship and pain, and real faith that will take you beyond the here and now into unimaginable peace, forever.

And may this Easter be your chance to have the "chance of a lifetime" fulfilled to your deepest core, just from knowing love won out over even the finality of death itself. And that it was an act of love directed straight at your heart.

I wish you a brilliant refreshed for life, renewed and strongly beating heart this Easter. To face every new day from this moment on with grace and peace and the assurance of something more, something to look forward to when your time on earth is through.

Some feel there are no absolutes and nothing is certain. I know that my Redeemer lives without a doubt. And that we too can not only live, but live victoriously beyond our human capabilities and means right here on earth, with renewal of heart. The renewal that comes from an absolute truth. And it is that we in our separation from God, who had nothing, who earned nothing, who merited nothing but the punishment of a forever broken relationship with the God who loves us, were redeemed back into God's good grace by a singular act in that Christ took our place, our punishment.

You can believe that or not believe it, but my heart tells me that act of love was absolute. That it was certain and not ever to be duplicated by any other living soul on earth. That it had a great and noble purpose, and that it was real. I believe it, and because I do, I wish for you a happy and revived heart this Easter, and a truly Happy Easter Day!

Chasing the Wind

Did you catch a piece of time in your hand?
Time that's full of laughter and love?
Time that's meant so much that you can scarcely think
about letting it go?
Thank God.
Did you catch a glimpse of joy as you looked?
Joy that's complete because you knew it was
heaven sent?
Joy that's so wonderful that everything else just
simply pales in comparison?
Thank God.
And what of life?
Did you learn to really live in your existence?
To reach out to touch the thorns as well as the
rose?
To fully enjoy living as each new day you met?
Then by all means,
Thank God.
Cherish these lessons of life well learned.
For too quickly time does pass.
And only what you do for eternity's sake
really matters, for it alone will last.
If you stopped to look,
and touch, and to love.
If you truly lived.

Well, did you?
- 1984 -

Living Garden

Lord,
do I produce blessing from
the rain that falls upon my land?
Or am I only producing thorns, thistles
and weeds?

Will the rain stop falling that washes
over me? That nourishes the seeds I plant?
Is my land in danger of being scorched and
rendered into ash and dust, never again to be
green and fruitful?

In the end will I have lost everything of my labor?

Have mercy on me, O Lord Jesus.
For I have not yet learned to completely
yield. Take this land of mine and plow through
the hardened rocky soil. Sift through the worthless
sand and dig out the useless clay and stone to
make it a fertile place where good seed may grow.

Where I may produce a crop of blessings that flow out
to feed the hungry world.
The starving hearts in need of you.
As I gaze this vast and unproductive plot of mine,
I thank you that
I do not work this land alone.

Hebrews 6: 7, 8

His Great Love

He climbed the lonely hilltop one labored step at a time.
Condemned without any mercy, love His only crime.
Surrounded by a throng of people but desperately alone.
His aching heart cried "forgiveness," if only they could have known.
It took the greatest love there ever was to hold Him to that tree.
It took the great forgiving love of Jesus to withstand this agony.

As they lifted him before the crowd, not once did He cry out!
The jeering mob grew restless and began to taunt and shout.
"If thou art the King...then save thyself," in mockery do they cry.
"Look at this messiah bleed, we all know that he will die!"

Jesus hung in sorrow and pain, seeing hundreds of souls in need.
"Tis not my will but thine my Father...these, are why I bleed."
One man in the hate-filled mob was pushed up against the cross.
With the blood of Jesus now on his own hands, would he realize the loss?
Did he proclaim what precious blood twas' spilled, or begin to understand? Or in disgust just curse this man and quickly wipe the blood from his hands?
It took the greatest love there ever was to hold Him to that tree.
It took the great forgiving love of Jesus to withstand this agony.

As Jesus draws His final breath those who love Him see,
that every tortured moment spent, was God's plan to set them free.
Do you search and seek out love dear friend? Then call on Him this day, and you'll begin to see.
That the greatest love there ever was, held Him fast upon that tree.
And it was the great forgiving love of Jesus, that withstood death for you and me.
- 1979 -

Dusty

He spoke of dryness Lord.
The long going on and on type that seems to never end.
But he couldn't sense the 'dryness to the bone' afflicting my life.
With it's cursed fingers gripping tightly to the core and very soul of me.
This is past mere dryness into "dust bowl, take your chances with a windstorm" dry. And part of me has blown on.
He also couldn't sense the 'loss of dignity' dry, which plunges head long into sin, not once, but often.
He spoke your word of warning when the dry spirit converts into a heart of stone. A hardened heart. I know it all too well.
He says that there are seasons of life. This is a season of dying back, dormancy. But unplanned, and unwelcome, unrelenting.
Dry makes one brittle to the point of break. Not a clean and healing brokenness mind you, but one which jags and fragments, and crumbles to the touch.
I'm glad he found the help he needs Lord.
Your sweet warm rain of grace to soften the hardened dry ground in his heart that he'd known...now turned into rich, fertile, pliable soil from which You can cause to spring forth multitudes of new growth.
But I sit.
Still parched and thirsting, desperately seeking, wondering.
Hoping that this dry spell does not drive out the living breathing hope. The promise.
The quench of spirit I've found in You.

Prompted by a message presented at Family Bible School by our Adult Class Speaker, Jim Medin June/89 -

Adrift

Life is set adrift
upon an endless sea.
Of unpredicted storms,
and strong winds of misery.
Is there not but one to bend
down low, reach out
and rescue me?
For surely I will perish,
in the deep blue, greens and grays,
of an ocean full of sorrows,
and dark skies that rule my days.
I am but a tiny speck that floats
upon life's awesome tide...
which keeps me fastened to this place,
from whence I wish to hide.
Would anyone please tell me,
where rest and comfort lie?
Or is it naught for the likes of me,
will no one hear my cry?
But just now as I lift my eyes
to see a patch of brilliant blue,
my help cometh from up above,
tis' God's help that's in my view.
To part the darkest gloomy clouds
and let the sun shine through.
No longer drifting I see the shore,
and my hope restored anew.
And life may well be set adrift
upon an endless sea.
But great His love which hastens
to rescue,
even one like me.

The Role

Upon the stage you play a part. The biggest of your life.
Exciting, invigorating, written just for you.
It has your feelings, your emotions, your passions, your flare.
It's the part you've waited for, dreamed of for all these years.
It's perfect, it fits you think. And it's what will validate you,
lift you up, make you...special.
The applause comes in ocean roars. Your fans surround you with
adoration and praise. After all, you're playing for them now.
Reaching into an empty place within to liberate, in as much as you
have already been liberated. The play ends. The stage is empty.
The people have all gone home.
Alone you sit before the mirror. Makeup comes off.
And you see yourself perhaps for the first time.

"It's just a part," your heart cries. "Why is it I couldn't see?"
Written, directed, and orchestrated with deadly intent unbeknown
to you, and played by many others before you. "What?"
you say..."I thought it was mine!" And how is it that others have
played this special part, written just for you?
The producer laughs a grim reminder. You've played the part of
a fool! The director, with binding contract in hand, waves a fond
farewell as your reality sinks in.

There is a master playwright. With your perfect part in hand. Who
sets the perfect stage, fulfills the passion of the part. And the other?
Only a sham. A short run glitzy production that no one seems to
remember at all. And to this day, they can't remember the leading
man's name. He stands in food lines now with the homeless, drifting,
and lost. Remembering all the missed curtain calls, as well as the
banquets, and the outstanding performances of all true artists within
the Master's Troop! It's not too late to ask Him, the part He holds for
you. Past performances don't count. He asks only that you come out
of the shadows, out from behind the curtain, and step into His
spotlight.

Choices

Would you take this nail?
It's not very smooth, I know.
And it's more like an old spike I guess you'd say.
Have you ever walked along and picked up
rusty old railroad spikes?
They are rough, crude, hard, dirty and cold.
Now walk over and take up the maul.
The hammer with which you drive the nail.
It's heavy and made to get the job done.
Your job lies ahead of you.

The Man.

He whom you embraced, accepted, and openly loved.
Who loved you back, who loved you...first.
Place the nail carefully. It goes between the thumb and the
outside edge of the hand. The base of the hand, if you will. You
want it to be secure. You want it to work, don't you?
To end this man's intrusion into your life once and for all?
Press the spike against your wrist...press harder. Try to imagine it.
Yourself - driven against the wood with this cold steel thing.
And hanging upon open throbbing wounds.
Have you suffered real pain? This Man's pain is His broken heart.
Because He's loved you so much. Because you said you loved
Him. Because...
you drove the nail.

There are two more nails to drive in, if one wasn't enough for
you. Just go pick them up. After all, nailing Him back up and
tearing His heart open once again seems a pretty simple task for
you right now. And when it's all over and done, the dirty job
complete, He'll die once again...but,

He'll still live on to love you,
even though you've rejected Him.
Though you drove the nails.
Though you choose death.

Choices.

We have so many,
yet so very few really. He had but one.
To love you.
So I'll ask again...
would you take this nail?

•

We all make conscious choices every day of our lives.
Some good, some bad. God's plan continues on no matter what
our puny decisions involve.

He really does not need us. He chose to love us and use us in His
plan. We can tear at His heart with every wrong choice at going
our own willful way in life, but it's never too late to turn back to
Him.

There's nothing that He will not forgive if we but ask in earnest.
He is the most compassionate, loving, patient being in all the
universe.

Our creator, and our purpose for being. And He forgives...
even when we 'drive the nails'.
March/87

Do You Wonder?

Does God exist?
Some may inquire,
and all I have to say is...

Can you design
a butterfly wing
or concoct the fragrance
of new mown hay?

Or take the humble
lightning bug
who sparkles on the fly.
Can you manufacture all
the parts
of this lantern in the sky?

Or can you fling a thousand
stars upon the dark blanket
that is night?
Or catch one such falling star
in a blaze of glory bright?

Nature sings of wondrous things
designed with so much care.
And a master designer who
cares for all, and counts
each numbered hair.

For He wrought mysteries
none can duplicate
or explain away as chance.
Far too intricate
are His works,
for mere happenstance.

So yes indeed, God does exist
and He made a plan.
To fellowship
with His special works,
especially with man.

So do not wonder anyone,
who set the sun in place to shine.
Or holds the seas at bay in shores,
of His own hands design.

Wondrous is His calling card, tis'
no mystery to me.
Miracles abounding
and round' them lie
and every eye can see.

If they but open wide their hearts
to accept the possibility.

•

O Lord, how many are thy works.
In wisdom thou hast made them all.
There is the sea, in which are swarms
without number. Animals both
great and small. O Lord,
thou hast made them all.

A Christmas Message

She had journeyed a far distance. It was uncomfortable and the road had been fraught with pits and stones which made it even worse for their traveling. She was tired. More completely exhausted than tired. Yet she hadn't questioned once the way chosen for her to trod. Joseph had received the same wondrous message concerning the new life within her. He would be "papa"and would bare the huge responsibility of mentoring the child who carried the knowledge of the universe within his heart, a thought that so many times would overcome him. How many questions Joseph stored inside himself, and what of Mary? She was very young, but looked far older than her innocence. She had experienced a miracle of no small proportion which would overwhelm even the most mature woman of the day. The longest journey for her, was just beginning.

But for now, it was a time to rest. She slept with her tiny infant son, forgetting the pain she'd just endured. The myriad's of questions and fears that swirled around in her head. She felt a strange and deep pang in her heart that could not be explained, which begged attention but gave way to the blessed quiet that came with gentle slumber. The new mown hay, pungent with smells of the stable, and yet oddly comforting to her for the moment. The lowing cattle and sheep were restless in their stalls, and it seemed such an unearthly place in which to bring forth a brand new, so fragile little life. Albeit, the life of a King.

She held in her arms a totally dependent little human being. A miracle. All births are miracles. But this time she was holding the promise of God. Not only a new life which held promise in and of itself, but new life for all mankind. For anyone...everyone.

She enveloped this tiny innocence in the arms of her love and slept. Perhaps it was the only time on earth when God genuinely felt the all encompassing love He so willingly gives to everyone, surround and secure Him, as a baby quietly nestled closely to His mama's bosom.

Mary..."mama." A love so closely akin to God's own that one wonders how it made God feel at that very moment. How often do we ever wonder how GOD feels?
It is that feeling that would be so long desired in mankind. That completely unselfish, warm and secure place where one could sleep without worry and care, entirely at peace knowing that more loving and capable arms held you.

That child, would be the one that offered to hold the world...so lovingly and securely and in just such a way. His birth would lead to the greatest act of love for anyone who would believe, for centuries to come. As we see young Mary cradle her tiny infant son, having given her last ounce of strength to bring Him safely into the world, we realize that many sacrifices both small and large have been made to assure us that God loves us.

He made the absolute and ultimate sacrifice to gather us close and surround and secure us in His loving arms. Christmas merits a closer look. Beyond the gentle and serene portrayals of the Savior's birth, there lies true struggle and sacrifice. Uneasy, unpleasant and harsh.

The ultimate "Yes!" to the affirmation of our very existence began with one such sacrifice. In a simple and unassuming stable filled with noisy animals, unpleasant odors, damp straw, and a simple peasant girl. Crude and humble beginnings for the greatest gift of love there ever was to mankind. Mary and baby rested there. And in the midst of our own unpleasant and crude stable experiences of life, may we also rest in His wisdom.

In His all-encompassing love for us. In His great act of
redemption of mankind for all generations, race, creeds, and
colors. In His warm and loving embrace, that feels like a mother's
gentle gathering us in close to her. For all time.
In the great expanse of time, and in the most troubling of times,
may you know this peace. Merry Christmas.

•

We See Love

When heaven weeps
we have rain.
And when there's joy
we see the sun above.

But when wooden
trees bleed from
broken sacrifice
and
thorny crowns replace
a rightful crown of
gold,

It's then...that we see
love.

Still Songs

Trees whisper over fallen comrades in nature's silence.
Pierced only with the occasional cries of birds jabbing at air.
I love this particular silence. Amongst debris of heavy laden beds
of wild grasses, branches, and living, dying life. If I advance, the
silence blossoms ripe with the crackle of dried leaves underfoot,
or the snap of tiny tree bones yielding to my weight.
And nature plays on it's harmonious lilts. Singing out for the
world to stop and hear. Whether we notice or not.
Most often not.

For the din of life has overgrown like bothersome weeds
inside our hearts and minds to block shut our ears.
As time, the great robber of men's essence, escalates it's
thundering demands for us to speed on and not look back.
The silence of nature sadly replaced with calamitous
meaningless noise. In a box, from a tube, on a chip,
like a head on a platter served with lettuce for color.
How dull and pale and hideous, when compared against
the backdrop of what's real and pretend.

Go gently into the woods my friends. Hear the wonders wrought
by God's own design. See the towering, flowing, graceful
monuments of silence and peace just waiting to be heard.
And to be felt, and inhaled...by all too ruined man.
"Too busy" you say. Well it will be there long after you've gone.
Still crying out for anyone to sing along. Perhaps the next one by
will catch it's yearning strains in a gentle breeze that one feels
softly against the cheek, and be wise enough to stop and finish
listening to the entire aria. The beautiful, haunting, melodic
sounds of nature's silence as it sings
it's still songs.

God Smile

It's in the quiet-tide
when gentle soft winds blow.
And shafts of pale light dance
with rustling shadows
swaying to and fro.
And earth takes in
a long deep breath,
a contented peaceful sigh.
To see the loveliness of
bright green grass amidst,
radiant white clouds aloft
yonder, in bluest of sky.

It's
A GodSmile.

True Solace

Your name is forever recorded in His book.
It can not be torn out, accidentally blotted out or defaced.
You are permanently His.
There are no obliteration's in God's Book of Life.
When you've become part of His river of life, you may flow
off into some small eddy or into a little tide pool somewhere
all your own, but...you are still a part of the greater body of
water that streams into eternity.
You are forever
His very own.

The Birthday

Tiny wiggling bundle.
Indescribable joy.
Living legacy of love
to follow, to teach, to let go.
Tiny wiggling bundle.
Incapacitating pain.
To live life on your own.
To reach, to search, to fall.
Tiny wiggling bundle.
Immeasurable love.
Living hope, living word who
wants to hold you fast.
To redeem, to restore and to heal.
Your beginning
has no end...and will
rescue us all.

•

As silently as the snows fall,
so came our greatest gift in silence.
As the single cry of a babe in a stable.
Whose arrival was heralded in
the hearts of simple sheperds,
and the starlit skies above when
the angels sang.
And still they are singing today.
And can be heard by any heart open
enough to listen just long enough
to catch them proclaiming,
that God's gift of love
has finally come.

The Bottom Line

Is not what you say, it's not what
you do. It's not what you know
or how long you've known it.
In the grand scheme of things,
anyone can call themself a Christian.
But it's calluses on the hands
that speak to the world.
And kindness of heart that shows
the world the
true heart of God.
What counts is "Who you know."

If you know Jesus personally
you're too busy to stand and judge
or evaluate the situation.
You just "stand in the gap" and dig in
and do whatever it takes, no matter who's
looking or keeping track.
God's record book is the only one that counts!
And if you are a Christian, you
don't have to shout. His love speaks volumes
even to those who can not hear.

Being a Christian today is not what everyone
else defines you to be, good or bad.
It's not a casual comment,
it's a lifetime commitment.
A novel in progress.

What's been written in your latest chapter?

The Sum of It All

And yet the sum of them, His eye
beholds but as a jot, a tittle, for he created them all.
We beat our chests and puff ourselves up with air from the
bellows of pride. And He looks down upon the earth and
considers puny man and how little are his accomplishments.
For man has yet to own the rights of peace, they have not set in
place an encompassing love that transcends the evils held deep
within their hearts. And they have not embraced the profound
truths of the One who holds them all in the palms of His hands.
All the lights of all the earth collected could not match the
brilliance of even one star that has been placed upon the blanket
of vast darkness that is the universe...by His own hand.

We "oooh and aaah" and marvel at all that man has achieved, and
yet do not appreciate the truly miraculous which can not be
manufactured or duplicated by our best efforts, no matter how we
try. We see the wonder of the world from a satellite picture poised
above us so far away, but can not find among the lot of us, a
singular heart in which the God of creation may comfortably
dwell.

While the world at large looks on in wonderment at things
which seem fantastic and great...I will slip silently away to study
the real things from which miracles are truly made. Like;
how a newborn's tiny fingers instinctively wrap around the finger
of the one who holds them close. Or, how to create a blade of
grass. What raw materials do I possess that did not come from
Him? I can not create something from nothing.
Every something must have a start.
Create in me a clean heart, O God...and renew in me a steadfast
spirit. That I may know my place. That I may see your face and
weigh true miracles in light of who you really are. And to help
me remember there is but one God who loved the world...enough.

What Can I Be Thankful For?

Sun and moonlight to light my days.
The lovely twilight with purple haze.
Comforts that others may not possess,
At the end of the day, a loved one's caress.
Peace that only God can give.
Strength renewed so that I might live.
A warm bed and pillow to lay my head.
A plate always full and a heart well fed.
With friends and family and love to spare,
And when extending a reach, a hand that's there.
Thanks for today because it arrived,
And for the troubles now past that I have survived.
For those whom I hold most dear to my heart,
And blessings that come of which they are a part.
Tender moments that come, even when they are few.
Time spent with friends, which of course includes you.
Thanks for this country in which we do live,
That says it's not better to receive, but to give.
And for the freedom that comes at such a great cost,
And prayers freely said that it would never be lost.
I am thankful as I look, and I sense and see,
Blessings small and large, whatever they be.
I can feel warmth when there's nothing but cold.
I can see beauty from ashes that transform into gold.
What in all the world over can I be thankful for?
God's goodness to me, Is there anything more?

May God bless you today and may you always find
in each moment of every day, something that makes you just
stop and say, "thank you."

107

Tears of the Heart

Tears of the heart are never seen
by anyone but God.
They are the pain that wrench the very
soul of us, and shake the foundation upon which
we stand.
They are that which come well after the others.
Counted - each one, and collected in His bottle.
They are those borne out of the loneliest and most
desolate places that our heart's and mind's can render.
Places untouched, untended,
until sorrow's intrusive moves upon our life
give them rule.
God guides the hand that caresses the ache, of every
tear stained heart. And gently lifts each wounded child
from sorrow's bondage into His peaceful presence and grace.
To a place where 'Heart-Tears' are, no more.
Psalm 56:8

•

A bruised reed He will not break, and a dimly burning wick He will
not extinguish - Isaiah 42:3

I wrote the above for the Leonard family and gave it to Janet
when Brad had been diagnosed with A-Plastic Anemia. The Lord
chose to heal Brad of this scary illness and restore him to full
health. A true miracle, as he almost died on many occasions and
many who have this disease actually do not live. I also gave this
to Judy Chambers of the Heart Center's Ornish program in 95' at
the death of her father. They had unfinished business at the time
of his passing.

Today

Today I'm up Lord.
I've seen a glimmer of the beauty of life
that too often went unnoticed before.
I thank you Jesus for beauty.
For too often in the every minute of living,
I've only seen the wreckage and ruin, and I needed
so desperately to behold your beauty
today.
And today I feel loved Lord.
Sensing your brightness driving the shadows of
despair far away from my heart.
I thank you Jesus for love.
For only a moment ago, loneliness almost surely
engulfed me from within the desolate place I stood.
And I needed so much to feel the warmth of your love
today.
And today, I think I can make it Lord...at least
one more hour anyway. Then possibly through the rest
of my day. I thank you Jesus for strength.
For the strength I need can not be collected and stored
for future use. But only kept one second at a time.
For the overwhelming, the unbearable, unthinkable odds,
I do need your strength today.
And Lord today, I feel like I belong.
The awesome measure of family, where once I seemed disjointed,
fragmented, and on my own. I have learned that I am more than
self...because you brought me in, collected me, and have given
me roots. I thank you Jesus for my adoption. For I needed to
know...
I'm yours today.

- for Janet, August/1988 -

Lessons Learned

Four to ten years in institutions
of higher learning,
studying the arts, learning the
disciplines,
preparing for life's ambitions,
has never been able to stack up
against the raw creative forces
that are welled up
within the soul of man.

He who has picked up the brush
and painted the world on canvas.
She who may
pen soul wrenching words
into well ordered prose
that evoke the passions of life,
from just living it!

These are the truly learned.
From which we can draw
forth our
greatest knowledge.

Your higher learning
is the world that surrounds
you.

No text book can teach us to feel.
Nor can they extract creation
from within
a warm
beating heart.

Compulsion

I must write!
In extreme urgency the pen wanders.
Bounding from thought to thought, not caring much
for time. Not really thinking, yet possessing a mind of
it's own with little consideration given to whether or
not things matter. Whether one can make
sense from all it's hapless meanderings
down
the
page.

Driven through the
processing of the mind's eye.
To write is to inhale...and then exhale,
to experience, and exist, and to think and feel and
cry out to a world too busy to notice.
It is the epicenter of every human tragedy,
at the core of every human soul, and
the cry of every human heart, ofttimes
compelled by God Himself.

Sing if you will.
Or dance your life away in the sway of time.
But as for me,
whether anyone ever
reads these words or not...
I must write!

The Art

(posted on a writing message board, revised here)

Absolute obedience to the gnawing within.
No force feeding of thought strewn haplessly about in what ends up as
nonsensical blatherings. The ones that are too often passed around as
enlightenment, or 'the latest in art noveau' or genius.
It's not pummeling the world at large with feigned, questionable talent.
"It makes no sense"... "Oh, you think not?"
"You've just no eye for real art." Perhaps, but only just enough to fool
the very elite, occasionally. And yet none of those things possess depth
nor meaning to the one who truly creates   . Those who pull up reserves
from deep within their innermost heart. Some people think, perhaps
more than they ought. And boast, more than we sometimes deem
bearable.
Their trademark accompanies them in their orange and yellow Pierre
Cardin' wraps, martini's in hand. They think they know, yet know
nothing. They judge and yet bristle if judged. They'd have no store with
such a blatantly under classed, presumed uneducated, or unsophisticated
lot. But wait just a moment. You can exalt the words that flow from your
creative calling as your ticket to real life. They enable you to be who you
are. They are, in and of themselves, the true art. The poetry, the
experience of breathing each day.

For those who stand upon the sidelines of creativity, who dare peer
through one-sided glasses and stifled emotion and haven't a clue, it's
simply this.

It is depth of one's soul spilled upon the individual pages of life
which constitutes real masterpiece. Stirring souls, saving lives.

Living is an art
That few execute well.

Chad's Poem - Summer Green

I wrote this for Chad Mike when he asked me to write a poem "just for him" one summer day. He was just eight years old. I thought of the beauty of having such a wonderful child and the blessings in my life. It was such a lovely sunny day and the green grass against the blue sky was awesome. It inspired this little poem "just for him." Green is one of the happiest colors in life, and I hope when he sees it, he'll remember this little piece and smile.

In the rainbow of colors that I have seen,
none has the beauty of summer green.
Cotton white clouds drift slowly by,
pillowy soft in the clear blue sky.
A myriad of brightness shines in
the yellow summer sun, but this
beauty can't cling to the one
of summer green.

Four Seasons

Summer's madness, joys and sadness mostly green.
Sun's hot, brown a lot, barely seen. Thus comes summer.
Autumn leaves, earth deceives, cold and hot together. Gently
drop, can not stop, rests gently like a feather.
Thus comes autumn.
Winter's cold, white unfold into billows bright. Once it comes
it shall return, silently through night. Thus come winter.
Spring's blooming, bees zooming, come what may. Sun now
shining, clouds lining, peaceful gathering day by day. Thus
comes spring...Thus comes life.

Bird Flu Casualties

Some folks have stopped feeding their Spring birdies due to the Avian Flu threats that they say "will be just a matter of time in arriving upon our shores." I personally think that's so sad. And although some would accuse me of living in the land of oblivion in light of such monumental issues, I can assure you that I do not. I just happen to refuse to allow, at this stage of my life, the almost daily dire warnings of impending doom, to rob me of some of life's simplest joys.

Each year we revert into anxious excited 'kids' with an attitude that is akin only to possibly waiting to open Christmas presents, as we await the first arrival of some of our beautifully feathered tenants. We see to it that we have an ample supply of seed (and of course there is corn for the squirrels as well as the Red Headed Woodpecker's, Cardinals and Blue Jays), sweet nectar for the brilliant Orioles and long-awaited Hummingbirds. We see that the Wren houses are up and in order, and prepare the small back yard pond for Frank (the frog) and his cohorts.

We can hardly wait to see the bright blue of the bunting and the 'yellowing-up' of the little finches. We rush to the windows, or stop dead in our tracks and hold our breaths at the breath-stealing beauty of these wonderful winged little creatures. And we get to watch their every effort to establish their summer homes.
And when the tiny Hummingbirds come, very soon after the Orioles (we think they travel on the same airlines, just different departure and arrival times)...we are elated! We just happened to see our first two Orioles earlier this week, and only yesterday caught two little hummers sipping from the Carlson soda fountain that is housed in the form of an overgrown plastic feeder colored and shaped like an orange with a green plastic leaf on top.

These little guys put smiles on dreary days and make stepping out into our tiny immediate back yard, a garden wonderland that I for one, am not willing to give up for the likes of the 'white noise' coming at me every day from media.

I am not closing my ears to things that I know I need to be aware of, I'm merely opening my heart to the wonders God hath wrought all around me. I can't imagine life without these simple little pleasures. And it breaks my heart to think that such a world could even exist without them. What with so much cruelty, hatred, violence, ugliness and suffering this whole world wide, I desperately cling to the tiniest bits of loveliness while I have them, knowing full-well that places like Darfur have virtually been wiped clean of them, from nothing less than man's inhumanity to man.

So finding our own bliss in our own little corners of the big world in which there exists many sorrows, and far too much darkness, is not only prudent but absolutely necessary.

So if you've come to a place where 'feeding your feathery friends' is in question, think of your world sans the lilt of their magnificent song. The incomparable color that we yearn to see from year to year and the happy feeling that washes over us, just because they've chosen to grace us with their presence another year.

They do not depend upon us, the food that we feed them, or the nectar and oranges we procure. We depend on them! Little feathered fluffs of assurance that come by each year just to let us know that life is still good for so many of us. That we can afford the luxury of a few moments of joy instead of the worry over what may come tomorrow.

God does see the sparrow that falls, and I know, especially when I am blessed each new Spring with fine-feathered little reminders, that He watches me.

Have you bought your birdseed yet?.

There's A Rose In My Garden

There's a rose in my garden.
Not so amazing.
Except for the fact the garden's been untended for years.
Thistles, weeds and wild grasses long since
homesteading on this small plot.
Nothing pretty to be seen there since, I don't know when.
But today,
looking out my window of loneliness,
I've spotted brilliant red
in the center of all reaching toward heaven.
It's a miracle of no small proportion.
The blue of the sky seems deeper now.
The green of the grass fairly glistens with
the newly formed morning dew.
White billowy clouds, which I'd foolishly
mistaken as gray before now, drift
high above the earth.
I hear beautiful notes from the birds singing
in the dense rich with green, tree limbs that surround me.
So often life seems long and relentless,
shadowed and bleak. Things long since forgotten, untended,
uncared for, amplify the solemn ticking of the clock.
Until
one day by myself, tea cup in hand, I look out my
window and discover...there's a rose
in my garden.

I gave this to Chris O. at a household shower given for her at my
friend Gertie's house June of 89'. This, after her and Roger's new
home completely burned to the ground and they lost everything
that they owned. I gave her this along with new Sanbakkelse Tins
with the original family recipe she had shared with me years
before that had been lost in the fire. (Which reminds me, I'm
gonna have to call her and hit her up for some of those wonderful
little cookies!)

Spring Thoughts

Winter winds shall blow on
to chill the hearts of others far away.
And the warm spring sun shall come to
awaken sleepy seeds and raise them up
to reach for it's bright rays, and remove their
heavy cloaks which kept them through the
long snowy night's slumber. And
once again, we will remember...t's time
to bloom again.

•

Sometimes after a long winter, we can
truly be thankful to see spring's little
indicators just around the corner. If you've had
what seems to be an insufferably long cold struggle, may
the winter of your soul soon give way to spring's lovely
promise in your heart.

•

Spring has almost sprung!
It's right around the bend.
The snowy cold and bitter winds
soon will finally end.
Sprouting buds and bits of color
awakening from a long winter's sleep.
Drawing warm sun from high above
and food from soft earth deep.
And just as days grow longer
and spring warmth fills the earth,
the birds will build, the earthworms glide
and small hoppers will add their mirth.

Trees standing tall and barren,
will sport new cloaks of merry green.
The sky will be it's azure bright
the prettiest ever seen.

I loved dear Winter's splendor,
it's quiet loving ways.
But I'm grateful still to see new life,
burst forth fresh
from new Spring days!

•

When we have stood in the shadows,
always behind, never out in the open,
and when we have finally stepped into the
glorious day and breathed our first real breath
of free fragrant life for the first time...
then and only then can we truly understand
gratitude of the soul.
Then and only then can we begin to know
what all the darkness was about,
and then and only then
can we go into the world
to illumine other darkened hearts.
- 2002 -

•

I never realized how fast the world
was spinning...until I stood still

I Had Forgotten I Could Fly

How long has it been
since I've felt so deeply?
Since I've truly tasted of
life's sweet pleasures?

Reluctantly, I step out to see
that the sky is azure blue,
and the effortless clouds still
hang in their rightful places.
The grass is greener,
the flowers brighter,
and yet my soul
is colorless.

Putting one foot
before the other,
my journey's forced and
become an unwanted labor.
And these eyes blinded
to the Sun's brilliant hope.

One day I will slowly emerge
from the darkened places of
this self-imposed cocoon.
I will brightly step into the morn
of an eternal hopeful day.

And I'll drink in the air
of fragrant joy.
And then remember

I have wings!

When we realize the significance of every human spirit, no soul can be entrapped, no heart considered hopeless, no limitations upon one's life imposed. And a word such as 'handicap' ceases to have meaning, and fails to exist in the hearts of men - lmpc -

The Dancer

She sat silently watching the other children play.
Hoping that she'd jump up and run to play with them one day.
And summer's came and then they went, and seasons were here and gone. Her youthful longings kept their pace as those children grew up and moved on.
Then as a young teenager balancing books with crutches in tow...
she still dreamt her dreams and endured the taunts that hurt her spirit so.
She was a pretty thing, and had a ready smile,
that betrayed the lonely saddened heart, which held no grudge nor guile.
She'd close her eyes and feel her feet gliding gracefully across the floor. Her auburn hair and bright blue eyes filled with hope, and more.
As the day approached, the big dance came.
She dressed her sunday best.
A most beautiful little wounded bird,
not quite fitting in with the rest.
Oh, how she longed for strong arms to wrap her tiny frame.
And sweep her up, let her feel loved, and 'normal' for a change.
She lived her life of solitude never abandoning that dream.
For in her heart of hearts she just knew, her prince would come one day to fulfill all that she had seen. And as upon her bed she lay, awaiting to draw her final breath, they all thought it rather odd to hear her laugh in the face of death.

For she was once more sitting in that lovely gown of lace. As
He gently took her fragile hand and lifted her in place.
He looked at her with loving eyes, so deep and very true. She
smiled and took his hand and said, "I've waited my life long
for you." Her Prince had come to rescue her. Said she
was the prettiest and fairest of all. As they danced across
the floor with grace at the angel's starlight ball.
She looked upon her Savior's face, and finally felt so free.
As she swirled and swayed and realized...
the greatest prince in all the world, from everyone,
chose me.

'The Dancer' was submitted to the 2theheart web site where it
was voted by it's world-wide readers as the poem of the
month with an award of $50. Then went on to become the only
poem that made it into the compilation of stories and poems
published in the book of it's namesake, *2theheart*, by web site
owner, Susan Fahncke. I was also voted the writer of the
month at that time by it's readers. Quite an honor for me in
light of the wonderfully talented writers associated there back
then, many who write for the 'Chicken Soup For The Soul'
book series. Some of these great authors may now be found
contributing their wonderful stories to my personal web site,
The WordSmith.

Tears
Simple terminology for expensive face-wash.

They seem to come at such a great cost to us.
And to those unfamiliar with tears,
who can't seem to cry,
if and when they do finally ever come to you,
they will seem the rarest commodity
that you've saved up
for your entire life long.

Unexpected Ambush

Years of bitter resentment just fell by the wayside. Along with the tears she wept. He had written her a love letter. He had never done anything remotely like that before through all those years.

She had steeled herself behind a wall of self protection for the want of never being hurt ever again. She'd been battle scarred, bruised, and painfully pummeled and left lonely. Oh, how she feared it...the loneliness.

And the wall began slowly, brick by brick. With an insensitive word here, an unloving act there. Heartache the mortar mixed throughout. The depth of pain suffered in rejection and loss from long ago, the feelings of inadequacy and meaninglessness. The kind that shouts at you, "you don't fit in anywhere on this earth!"

All the baggage she brought into this relationship she brought with heavy resolve. And she'd made her stand. And anger turned into unkindness, and unkindness into hatred, and hatred then, into indifference. All symptoms of hurts long gone and too unattended to. Accumulated through years of passionless life and dreams unfulfilled.

She couldn't remember a time of warmth from her cold and hardened heart. But all it took to make the wall come crashing down, was a simple letter. Not eloquent or flowery, but real. Which simply stated that, "he truly loved her." And that she was the most important person in his life for all time.

And here she sat. Weeping great sobs of overwhelming tears
which washed over her whole being, like a cool and gentle rain.
Cleansing away in waves of great release, the bitterness, hatred,
and sadness.

Words...when spoken, must be chosen with care. Years spent
carelessly flinging them out here or there with no thought, had
accumulated into huge heaps of worthless rubble and ruin in her
life. Only to be cleared away in an instant. Miraculously.
With a few penned from his heart.

Soothing, reassuring, and reaffirming her value.
As a woman, a person, a beloved wife, for whom there was love
and purpose. How very long she'd waited to just "feel"
cherished... if even for just a moment. And how often she had told
herself that she hadn't really cared, and that it didn't really matter.

All the bitter facade now vanquished, she had been softened and
broken by simple words on a page.

Golden and treasured. She consumed them all.
And let each one take residence in her heart.

The siege had ended.
The wall was down.
The reserves sent packing.
As she opened her heart and
her arms for the very first time,
to love.

Stones Upon The Ocean

O, the pull of mighty waves whose power has calmed
to gently brush the shores in timeless effort.
Reaching across miles of promise and bridges of dreams.
Hope stands upon the shoreline readying for a sign.
An eternal - internal prompter to stand firm and never waiver.
Ancient tales reach lands end as broken bits of a puzzle unsolved.
A sweetheart's promise, stored as an undiscovered pearl
buried in the sand, a treasure yet awaiting to be found.
Will this moment last?
Not long enough.
Will the good of life outweigh the heartache?
Unlikely so.
But as strong and sure as waves that reach the destination of their
desired journey, so shall all life bridges have to be crossed.
And as long as hope stays, love of life will triumph and endure.
Just as the mighty ocean waves.
And our hearts will serve
as the skipping stones.

(Written for Jazzie's Studio Web Site)

Jazzie is a talented artist who does water colors and sculptures to make
beautiful collectable art. She also suffers with CFS and Addison's Disease.
Please pay her a visit. HERE: http://www.jazziestudio.com/paint.htm
You will be blessed to see her efforts despite the pain and struggle of
chronic illnesses she must endure. And her lovely art is for sale. I am pleased
that she has sold some of her beautiful paintings through our efforts at
Writer's Block and our CFIDS/FMS Support Communities.

Small Legacies

Every family has them.
In a book, on a table.
In boxes up on the shelves of closets.
Little squares of life captured, for just a moment.
Held for a lifetime.

Faded shades of gray or brown, or colors
now melded together in untrue to
life memories.
The edges are tattered or bent, or missing.
Just like the people they represent
from a land of faraway.

Pictures. So happy-so sad, and
so far removed from those who dwell within them,
and those now residing on the outskirts of these
lives once lived.
So much meaning behind each one.
For they meant something to someone,
sometime ago.

Why do we place such importance in the tiny
square pieces of paper of these images captured?
In time spent hundred's of lifetimes ago?
With a breath of familiarity warm against
our faces, a whisper asks...
"Don't you recognize me?"

Thread of life
throughout the ages
has come to this.
Has come to...this.

Clean The House

(for Judy Johnson Heckman and Dale upon their move to
Texas/1990 - one of the saddest times of our lives, losing good
dear friends to such a long distance between us)

Clean the house.
Yes, it's time. Sorting, organizing and tossing out that which no longer
serves us well. Open wide the closets and cupboards. Dig through the
contents and set aside the things you're unsure of...
then move on.
Reach into the corners, dust off the shelves, carefully wrap the memories as
cherished keepsakes you must take with you. Delve deeper and you'll find
loving friendships that can not be left behind. And look at this!! An almost
forgotten moment rediscovered! How wonderful to find such treasures as
we labor to clear out old for new.
And here sits a relic of great proportion. How could it ever be replaced,
and with what?
It's going to leave a place for all to see, where time has worn all around it.
A lasting reminder that it once stood in this very place. And look what
came from this corner of remembrance, we could never throw this away.
No, we'll just have to take it with us when we go.
The heavy task gets lighter as we move from room to room. But each
newly opened drawer stirs waves of recollection, as we pack up time well
spent. So many pictures to put away. Some fun and some sad, but all
important as we carefully tuck away each one.
Sometime we'll drag them out again and laugh, and cry, as we long for
long lost days.
Place a few preserved moments of 'loving thoughts between friends'
inside. These are things that will have to travel along with us as well.
As we look around and begin to see the empty rooms and places of the
heart, we realize that with the careful sweeping, it does seem to leave a
very vacant place.

But we remember the bustle of activity here, the well worn arm chair holding one friendly face after another there. The laughter, the singing, the rejoicing, the real contents that made this place our home.
Still we must...clean the house.
From top to bottom, inside and out, not a single moment to remain. To stand silent and waiting.
A spotless 'new beginning' to learn, to discover, to create. And every so often we'll think of what was left behind, it's noble frame which held us safe through many-a-storm. Whose walls echoed sounds of love and joy, and laughter...always laughter.
And we'll smile at the thought. And we'll look through the carefully packed boxes to see what we can find to help make the new place "home."
And we'll be thankful.
And when the broom stands idle in the hallway, it's job complete at last, when new occupants arrive, they'll see a clean house. With not a hint of the life once lived within. The walls well scrubbed, shall not tell of the love shared here with friends. Of the family who grew in grace here and became permanent fixtures in our hearts. The 'hidden treasures' in every corner shall go unseen by the untrained eye.
But we shall remember it all.
Every nook and cranny. Every weathered piece of wood. The familiar creaks when you walk across the floor, shall not escape our memory.
This was a home.
Well lived in.
Where memories can not be washed off,
nor any amount of 'elbow grease' ever scrub away the years.
And knowing this, we must now begin...it's time,
to
clean the house.
(July 6th, 1990)

Dale, Judy, Kristie, Julie, and Kellie Noelle's last day with us as pastor, friends, family...was July 22nd, 1990. They enriched our lives and added such joy, and we still miss them even today, all these years past...very much! May God keep and protect and always richly bless the Johnson-Heckman families.

Time Squeezed

How time enamored are we all,
and scurry around do we.
To accomplish oh, such tiny feats
in light of eternity.

How well scripted are the days
that pass so quickly by.
To fade so fast into obscurity
in a life that's but a sigh.

I wake to face another day
with scheduled lists for every minute.
With no regard to live life fully
and see the beauty in it.

No time to stop and hear the sound
of angelic chords being played,
or catch a whiff of the blooming rose
so regally displayed.

Oh, that I could lay upon the sea of
grassy green and linger in the moment,
for just a moment more.
Or find a starfish buried in the sand
upon the sun-washed shore.

But time demands my every inch,
a mad task master is he.
And small are my accomplishments
in a vast eternity.

Write Your World

I write my world.
From behind the confines of flesh covered walls
and red coursing words, through veins of passion
and rivers of fury.
With due passage of time and circumstance,
it does ebb and flow, and crest and break.
I stand upon the very edge of life
poised for the dive
into oceans of the unexplored.
Most inviting, yet I hesitate to take the plunge.
And what is it that hold the feet so firmly?
Fastened...immovable to this inch of earth
upon which I stand?
What is the fear that robs me of the anticipation
of living out life's untold joys and limitless promise?

I write my world.
And yet words fail to launch the escape from
these things that bind, and that will not free the spirit
which longs to sail over uncharted waters.
With feet chained and arms outspread, facing the
winds of challenge, head back, eyes closed...
feeling the vast expanse of life outstretched before me,
I hear the whispered admonishments from the gentle breezes
blowing acrost' the soul...

"You write your world."
"You stand poised and ready for the plunge,
but the word you are searching for to begin
is...jump!"

The Dryness of Being

Pray tell,
why is it that some days I
awaken to endless fields
velvet deep in words? Thick, rich, plentiful,
flowing gracefully forth to brighten the darkest
valleys of mediocrity and the mundane?
And other days I stumble.
Parched and thirsting for but one drink of the life
giving, pulse-restoring quench of words that will
carry me through the cracked and eroding
deserts of drought deep within my heart?

When the well runs dry and the pen is silent,
the soul crumbles.

More To Life

When you dream, dream in color.
When you laugh, laugh out loud.
When alone or feeling lonely,
seek the fellowship of kindred hearts
in the crowd.
For today is but a single breath,
tomorrow yet a dream.
And life the fine art of gathering
simple blessings in between.
So catch them each one, while you may.
Love more, sing, laugh and play.
Do not fade silently into
night's deep mists,
without really
living on the way.

Love Allocated

I had a gift bestowed with care
upon my heart, most cherished there.
But I sensed this gift would greater be,
should I share my gift unselfishly.

I set about to find a way
to share this precious gift today.
I found this place with souls so dear,
Best served my gift, I'll leave right here.
Encouragement to one trouble heart,
kind words to another was a pretty good start.
But time found my giving lessened some,
as daily to this place I'd come.

Too often the gift I would hide away,
so freely entrusted to me that day.
For in one I found words that chaffed my soul,
so from that one, my gift I'd withhold.
In still another I sensed an attitude unkind,
and harsh words then followed, I would find.

And so there it lay, my treasured gift.
I could not just leave it in their midst.
So quickly I steeled my gift away
and clutched it close to my heart to stay.
But the greatness we're given,
we must greatly use, or such precious gifts
we stand to lose. So do not withhold your love
and care, thoughtfully given for you to share.
Instead of losing love's gift so true, unwrap
your heart, the gift is you.

Too Close For Comfort

I don't like sharing myself.
The me that's inside
that comes tumbling forth.
Forming words in an all too personal way.
I don't like anyone getting close enough
so as to suppose by reading me in these lines,
that they know who I really am.
I like my distance.
My anonymity.
The lines on paper with no face or name.
For my arms-length can keep at bay
all who would come to realize
that within the contents of these works,
there beats
a true and living heart.

The Almost Friends

I proceed with caution.
They draw nearer.
Will they mean to harm or
will I be carelessly abandoned,
rejected, just when my heart is bared?
Quickly I fear...and run to hide.
The wall goes up
and once more I retreat.
Not one is ever the wiser.
And my soul cloistered,
yet awaits discovery.
And they have come the
closest ever to knowing
who I really am.

Window

There is a little window
I look through every day.
Where I view many of your loved
ones Lord, that prompt this heart to pray.
It's a window that you gave me Lord,
that transcends all time and space.
To recognize each hurting soul
by name and not by face.
How simple as I sit and look,
and upon each name I gaze...
to voice a little prayer for them,
that you might brighten up their days.
I don't fully know them Lord,
but you fully know each one.
Every heartache, struggle, dream, desire,
each life that's come undone.
Every crisis-need that is expressed,
and the ones that never are,
are seen and heard and understood
from your window from afar.
Thank you for my window Lord.
Help me make it one of prayer.
As I sit and view each name you love,
remind them that you're there.
You may wish to speak your gentle words
of understanding kindness from above,
today through my little window Lord,
in the way I "speak" your love.
April 2001

•

It occurred to me how very simple it would be to extend a 30
second prayer for each name I see online in a day. Thirty seconds

may not seem much, but much can be said in that time. If you don't think so, give yourself 30 seconds to compose an e-mail or post on a message board to see just how "long-winded/worded" you can actually get! I can write a lot in 30 seconds time.

By applying the 30 second principle, I will have spent about 5 minutes in prayer for 10 different people! And for 10 minutes, I would have covered about 20 people etc. and so forth.

In doing so, I would have invested less than an hour of time that normally I would have spent dispensing my own "so-called" wisdom and wit to at least 100 people, instead, asking God's direct intervention into their 100 lives, a far better use of time as I see it. Of course after the hour's up, I can go back to my astute wisdom dispensing modus operandi, ha!

I believe in the power of prayer (most assuredly), and in the God who listens and answers. Not always as we'd like or expect, but always with the best interests of those He loves foremost at hand. I am a 'pray-er', and I expect things to happen when I pray just because God said that we could expect that they would happen. I would far rather prefer God's perfect wisdom and guidance into my loved ones and friends lives than having anyone lean on my puny understanding and "wisdom" any day.

So, as you go online today...
think about applying the 30 second principle and just
see how it blesses not only the lives of those names
on the screen in manifold ways, but also yours as well.
Go ahead...just open the window!

Walking The Rim

Tottering along the edge.
Arms spread wide to steady
as one step is placed upon another.
Sometimes eyes opened wide, then closed.
At others, intently watching
so as not to falter.
Around and around we travel.
Encircling world upon worlds of dreams,
and heaps upon heaps
of ashen promise
ready to be scattered with the wind.
Should we stop - or
venture onward to destinations yet ahead?
Have we lost our way?
Time worn grooves rut life's pathways too often.
We remain on the rambling sphere
where comfort means traveling the sure footed route.
The kind that becomes all the same.
The one where blindfolds are easily worn
and one will always end up
back at the start.
Because the grooves never change.
I take a breath.
I step outside.
Peer over the precipice
and let the blindfold fall.
And finally stop
to take it all in.
This all encompassing
new view of life,
walking the rim.

No Such Prejudice

We dance to the tune most macabre
upon earth's floors betwixt the bitterness and sweet
and the unimaginable.
We've walked, each one, into our own appointed lots in life.
Some ran crazy with fear, others with hatred exuding from
wild angry eyes and pounding fists.
In the horror of their acts, the laugher's screeched with delight
at the deeds their demons had done.
So out of place, this laughter,
amid such a pitiless mob.

The graves will hold the evidence, just as in the years past.
And when finally unearthed 200, 700, or a thousand years from
now...
all bones will still be white.
Silent testimonies which will betray whether the flesh which
once held them together was either black or white, or
Christian or Atheist, Catholic, Muslim or Jew.
And the savor of their long lost lives never more determined
by the corrupt eyes of evil puny man.

The tombs of men, where the dividing lines of prejudice and
hatred end with nothing more or less
than rock-hard whitened bones.
Life itself does fly in the face of the maniac's rumblings, when
wounded in wars of separation.
There is yet to be found pulsing through the veins of
humankind, any blood that is not red,
and
we all do bleed.

And are bloodied by destitute and bankrupt souls in
misguided battles raging.
Against ghosts long since dead and sins buried deep within the
hearts and souls of men.

Search long and hard, oh players of the night.
For judgment day will one day come for you.
And all those things lying hidden in the depths of your soul
will be revealed in all it's ugliness.
And God,
looking out across the battlefields of these bleached white
bones, will see yours black and turned to dust.
For far beneath those blood stained pastures you'll cry out for
Him to take you home, and in agony you'll look up only to
read the sign that in heaven says,
"NO SUCH PREJUDICES ALLOWED"!

LinQuotes

•

The world may never see
the hidden worth of a single heartbeat.
But each is counted and numbered
by the One who sets in place,
the metronome of life and breath.

•

All of life is propaganda.
The only reality comes from
the truth within the heart.

Exile

Walking...
with no possessions, into worlds' unknown.
Fear and anxiety hovering above.
Ominous smoke filling the air, burning the lungs
as life translates into death, meaning translates into madness.
The eyes betray the moving forms.
Dead eyes gray and wandering, frantic in their search
for something, anything that would scream "this is a mistake"
of the most monumental means!
The exhausted keep walking, laboring one step at a time.
The mind long numbed to pain, oblivious to what's real.
The treasured things of which life consists
now left behind as dust. Was it all merely a dream?
The love, the kindness, the laughter, the life?

Mamma had remembered that she'd scolded Peter just the day
before for waking Papa with all his childish noise.
Why had she thought it so important then, when now Peter
has fallen off the face of the earth forever?
He was just a small sprig of a boy whose mamma and papa are
now gone from him and...he must be so afraid.

No one spoke or dared to.
Just walked this endless walk. Haggard, fevered, sick, broken
and bewildered. As if stepping into a time-warp, into places
cruel and heartless, and nowhere near
love.
And then...
those burdened feet stop at their final destination.
One made of vast stone gray walls and fences.
So many fences.

Too dangerous to climb.
Barking dogs, fierce and angry and in a frenzy.
And human eyes, hungry for any sign of disruption or
disobedience from this forlorn group of refugees come so far
from home. For such acts could instantly be interpreted as
independent human will, not tolerated by these snarling,
furious, crazed and hate-filled eyes.

One could be shot for such things as this or worse,
allowed to live here...in this desolate and unfamiliar hell.
And many did dwell among the lunatics mad with power and
completely void of spirit. And among the frailest wisps of
flesh and bone, the walking dead.

We must not forget.
No, we must not ever forget.
For the fine line which exists between life and death,
between you and me and the side of the line upon
which we stand, that differentiate between the lunatic
destroyer and the purveyor of love and life,
too often is crossed so easily by
the single footstep
of
just
one.

A Holocaust reminder. A madness remembered.
A shame which should resonate into eternity
and never be allowed again.

And just remember that every time you hear
the words "ethnic cleansing" in the news, this is
exactly what is taking place. And is still being
allowed to take place today in parts of our world!
Lord, have mercy on us all and change the hearts of men!

Little Eyes Broken Heart

When We lose Our Humanity
We Have Forever Lost The World - lmpc

I had seen one picture after another. My ears had heard multiple accounts of horror and sorrow from this one woman and then another man. Relayed with such deeply felt emotion that it shook them to their very soul.

Man's inhumanity to man, is what's it's often referred to. But the intensity of the cruelty played out, the unspeakable, unfathomable atrocities just have to be thought of in darker, heavier, more raw and ominous terms.
And maybe there just are no words that exist which would quite describe the plight of millions at the hands of mad men, in the then considered intellectually advanced society known as fascism.

Nazi Germany.
Who could begin to imagine the wave of abject putrid rot that would waft it's way across that land to corrupt and destroy the lives of so many innocents? That would cause common man and woman, to close their eyes and ears to the obvious genocide surrounding them, visible daily to them, sometimes even coerced and goaded on by them?

I must admit that even today, in all my 56 years of living, I still fend off feelings of extreme revulsion and bitterness towards German people. For allowing such things for so many years. For actively participating in the merciless and vile acts perpetrated against people for nothing more than one wild-eyed lunatic's bent and distorted ideals. How could they allow such a thing? How could they DO such a thing?
The Holocaust.

In all of the visual assaults I've ever seen of that time, one in particular broke my heart into a million pieces.

It was of a child. Obviously Jewish, possibly from one of the ghetto's set up for Jewish people of that day while they awaited in sickness, want, and squalor, to be pushed farther into the oblivion of the death camps 'when the time was right' for them to be herded like cattle, deprived of all that is the most basic of human needs, tortured, then executed without a second thought, without a tear of regret or remorse.

He was standing alone.

Looking at someone that obviously deemed it fit to take his picture right then. It wasn't a still picture. You could see his dirty face and disheveled clothing. But the thing that cut me to the very core was his countenance. His little face looked as if he were trying so hard to bring up some sort of a smile, but he just couldn't quite muster it. All while his eyes harbored glistening tears that waited yet to fall. His eyes sparkling wet and pleading, his mouth trying to smile but forced into what seemed a look of desperation and yet hope all at once, which pierced my heart and made me cry.

What had those little eyes seen?

Where was his mama and daddy? Did he see something so awful that his little heart ceased beating at just that instant? Had he ceased to be the child standing before us at the very moment this picture was being recorded for all of time, so that history from then on could see it and wonder about him forever?

Those eyes, that face, emblazoned into my mind and my heart forever! In tears and brokenness, I wanted to leap through the television screen and scoop him up and just hold him.

Rock him gently to sleep and caress his brow and comfort his sad little heart and make his terror all go away.

And to this day I wonder about that little sorrow-filled face. Did the monsters get him? Did they hurt him to the extreme? Did heartless soulless so-called 'men' stand by while terrible things happened to that sweet innocent soul?

My heart still aches for a boy that, had he survived any of the nightmare unfolding before him, would far be my senior in age, and yet...in my minds-eye, in my heart, he is still and forever that sad little lost boy.

And where does that picture that broke my heart leave me today? Were I to allow the swell of hatred to grow against the perpetrators of such evil against babies and innocent lives, would I not be one just like them?

I fight such feelings every time I see the next documentary, hear the testimonies of those who were forced to live out nightmares while awake and walking on planet earth, in a place the likes of which hell itself could not rival. Whose families were callously murdered one by one before them, who lost track of every touch of humanity, every touch of dignity a person could have, who lost every ounce of kindness they had ever known, and virtually lost their sanity in the mad house run by lunatics and demons straight from the pits of hades.

Oh, dear God...help me to be kind.
To spread kindness and grace to all. If I fall in the wake of a monstrous tide that sweeps away innocents across my land, then let me be found among the innocents. Hopefully with strength enough to grab the one that's hurting standing right next to me, and hold them close...no matter their color, race, creed, lifestyle, position, religion, or class. And please, have mercy on us all. We do not, in our inhumanity, deserve it. Your mercy or your grace. Even the best of us - at our very best.

Oftentimes the best of us can fall, we can fail under the right circumstances. Help me to try to remember that, when I see the little broken heart pleading from behind the eyes of that hurting small boy.

I pray for this to never happen again. I pray concerning the sin which has festered the wickedness in men since the beginning of time that brings about such evil against others, to be once and for all defeated, and for all men to see the condition of their own hearts.

Their own heart condition, which is tied directly to their immortal soul. The one in which there is no hope or escape outside of repentance and deliverance by the God whose heart too, has been broken by the tears of a single child. Have mercy on us all.
We would all do well to remember, lest we reap the repeat of what's been sown in evil seed through centuries of allowed tolerances, by those too indifferent to care.

I wish with all of my heart that just one would have cared enough to spare the sorrow, the torture, the sadness of that one broken little boy that haunts my days.

If I could only see him today, even if he were eighty years old I would ask, "Are you all right little soul"? Because these things are imprinted in the heart as permanent snapshots that are taken in by the sensibilities and mechanisms of a small child. Forever engraved there. To be reviewed by that child's heart who took them, even if that child lives to be eighty or a hundred years of age. And just was he to be all right?
I guess I will never know.

•

Sorrow is the invisible force that binds every soul whether
we know one another or not. Those who have experienced it have an
instant kinship with the unfamiliar face of
anguish that lives across the ocean.

Eyes Of The Innocents

Peering out from tiny faces.
Some with tears, some without...too numb to feel.
Little souls stripped bare to the bone without a
second thought, without compassion.
Little souls left to wander the earth, void and
emptied of all their innocence.
Who can say a prayer that will be heard for these
tiny, oh so so sad eyes we see each day?
What dear God, can mend hearts
so ripped and torn apart?

War.
All mankind hates it.
All mankind craves it, and the gates of hell
applaud it and revel in it's wake, the little lives to take.
Will no one stop the course of this incessant rage? To
restore a smile? To build a child with hope,
dreams and laughter?
To once more gaze upon the tiny faces filled with
wonder and love, and life?

Cold death I pray, will slink away in defeat.
And cold hearts, lovers of war...be forever banished
to the nether worlds from
whence they came.
Never to be seen again by little
eyes
so sad as these.

What Evil This?

What is this pungeant evil wind
that blows across the land?
Which takes the breath of decency
away from common man?

Which begs the last morsel of good
that beneath life's table lies,
and uses forceful acts of madness, leaving
a land where love and kindness dies?

And bends the limbs of tolerance to break,
and turns every heart to stone.
Forcing innocence from every soul
to leave them desolate and alone.

This evil that men dispense on earth,
will likewise follow them to hell.
The crimson evidence shall arise
to create a tidal swell.

Which will engulf them in it's wake.
To drown their evil schemes.
What's been metered out on earth by them
Shall consume them so it seems.

Defy the evil ways of men
and stop their wicked days.
Turn this evil tide for good
or perish in their ways.

Ugly World

I don't like the world in which we live.
It is an angry ugly place.
There is a seed of insanity embedded
that has slowly seeped into the soil of life, to infect it's
inhabitants as it grows and pollinates it's deadly intent.
An innocent five year old Iraqi boy was set on fire by a band of
masked and cowardly deviants. What did this child do? Such a
hideous act of violence perpetrated. This terrified, traumatized
innocent little boy who survived only to face the pain and suffering
inflicted upon him surgery after painful surgery, nightmare after
relived nightmare, from such an act of atrocity! May God have
mercy.

Monsters walk this earth. Demons from the very pits of hell are
loosed! They do exist! Look at that child's horribly disfigured face
and tell me that it isn't so!

Or perhaps the babies of Darfur. BABIES less than a year old who
were ravaged along with their mothers and sisters, then cast onto
garbage heaps with the broken bodies of those left to suffer and die.

They also walk in the form of the 'civilized' who bear their children
only to rear them a few short years for death. Strapped into the back
seat of cars and pushed into the river, wide-eyed with terror while an
'un-mother' slowly watches them sink to their deaths.

This world where the "elite" are out in the forefront and in the
public eye, and are exalted above the rest of 'common ordinary man'.
Touted by media moguls as being the someone's that matter...the
better class, those who are so over paid for so little effort in life, who
"have it all" over those who have precious little. The rich, the
famous, the achievers, supposedly the only ones to listen to, not the
small and "insignificant" common workers who daily, without
fanfare, make the world tick.

146

Those who make the cogs turn, and save lives, and keep things running smoothly by quietly doing their underpaid and thankless drudge work w/out complaint, day after day after day, unnoticed by all but those who love them best.

The First Responders, EMT's, Letter Carriers, Bank Tellers, Steel Workers, Nurses, Soldiers, Truck Drivers, Grocery Workers and hundreds of other unsung heroes who do their jobs and obey the laws of the land and strive for better lives by reaching out to others and doing what they can. Whose skills often times determine life or death situations in an instant, whose hard efforts sometimes place them directly in harms way for the sake of their family and others. Who's difficult work keeps this country vital and functioning. Whose salaries barely keep them going or able to sustain their families. We are way off-balance with what's important here and who it is that we should be looking up and listening to.

I don't like the world in which we live. Where freedom once had been the highest ideal and most enduring motto of this land. Had been the earmark of who we are as an individual nation. That now has come to exalt and perpetuate individual personal freedoms as the single most important right over constitutional rights, dictating just how much freedom each individual may possess by the amount of noise and ruckus made by one over another. Where opinions are held in higher regard than the freedoms we have to even own, or to voice them freely.

A world where God supposedly (according to many), condones hatred, violence, and barbarism that stems from religious zealotry and forced impositions of beliefs against others. Believe it or die is their motto. A world where freethinking is unacceptable, where one can not really have a thought of their own. Where sexual sins such as adultery, or what is tantamount to stealing by certain religious sects by pleading for donations that keep them living well above the poor folks sending them in, that keeps them building their version of religious Disneyland, can be absolved with a few seemingly heartfelt tears and a genuine performance of sincerity and contrition.

147

A world where the word "SHAME" has ceased to have any valid meaning at all. There is no reason to even keep this word in the dictionary. It is archaic. It has ceased to exist for modern mankind. That sole prompter of our souls which leads to in-depth inner searching to reach a better us. That may just lead to a repentant lifestyle or self discovery which turns our heart around. That turns the world around to do better.

I don't like the world in which we live. Where the only way to be heard is to argue. Where kindness has been consumed by greed and selfish concern. Where generations are totally lost due to busyness and broken spirits.
Where love is no longer recognized for the lust that has taken it's place.
Where 'family' is obsolete, or open to interpretation by the 'more learned' scholars, instead of what it actually is! Two parents who genuinely love and care for and are actively involved and interested in their children's lives, their futures and well-being.
Where Senior Citizens are shipped off to death-homes that are commonly referred to as Nursing Care Facilities, so that they can get on with the business of dying and getting out of the way, instead of being lovingly respected and cared for by people who treat them with the dignity they deserve. Who are not lauded for their years of service, wisdom, contributions and expertise of a lifetime, but tossed aside like yesterdays trash. Where personal dignity is stripped away and most often left at the doorway as they enter in.

A world where my God, who has given me everything, who has laid His life down for me, can be misrepresented, misinterpreted, maligned, mocked, blocked, banned, kicked around and poked fun of in any way by anyone without so much as one indignant remark of offense allowed from me or those who believe as I do, without becoming labeled a fanatic, lunatic fringe, know-nothing, backward, uneducated hick. Without being made fun of, or given a tag that spells 'dangerous radical religious right' upon it.

A world where the common man is trapped in a bubble that rolls along as we run our legs off trying to keep up. To keep feeding the greedy appetites of insurance companies and major corporations and pharmaceuticals and big businesses that grip the land. We are insurance poor, overtaxed and under represented and just uncared for. All while the monsters, thugs, thieves and murderers are free to plunder and lay waste, and the "elite" party on, unconcerned.

I don't like the world we live in.
It has long become an unfamiliar, cold and lonely place. Where unkindness reigns. The Bible tells us that we are merely sojourners/visitors, if you will, just passing through. This is not our home. And for that fact alone, I am most assuredly grateful.

For in this place of unwelcome, this 'stopping off place' in the journey, I will never be so thankful as when I reach my final destination place away from here. Until then my prayer is simply, "God, help me keep that final place in sight long enough to just continue on, while I must be here."
To be able to try to hold fast to love, not the hate that this world spawns. To have the desire to love and reach out to those who make my traveling so much harder than it has to be. To work at forgiveness, not take in and hold on to the bitterness from it all.

I don't like the world in which we live, but help me to remember Lord, that you lovingly made it all, and that You yourself are love.

We need your direction, your guidance, and we desperately need you to help us reach with love toward others, so that we may see what life could be. That we might live to see the fruits of that love transform the ugliness of this world into the beauty you'd intended it to always be.

I don't like the world in which we live.
Help me Lord,
to try to change it!

Manifest Destiny

He calls to the mountain.
It's stately presence a monument
of ancient wisdoms
passed down through the ages.
To stand through the echoes
and voices of long ago,
of the past.
What would this silent aged
wonder say to us today?
"Oh man, take heed of
thy maker's intent!"
"All the wonders of
this earth were made for
His pleasure."
And yet, foolish hearts
dwell at odds with their
one hope of life's real
purpose.
To make Him
known,
and manifest
His love to all.

•

When you live, you love.
When you love, you risk it all.
And when you lose love,
you sometimes never want
to take the risk again. But you will.

- placed at New Zealand Grief and Loss -

150

Forevermore

She stood in darkened silence,
overlooking all that was.
Her feet still felt the memory
of the tall grasses in the glen.
The soft wind kissed her cheeks,
as the sun began to rise.
Only the glint of the early risin' sun
would catch
the tears
fallen from her eyes.
For her wee lad would not be comin' back...
her sweet lips to kiss again.
Echoes of better days gone by,
laughed across the glen.

She heard his voice remind her,
to gently lay this burden down.
"For no wars, nor fightin' there ever was...
could ere' take him from her heart."
"I'll be your strength," said he.
"As the days ahead you'll
face, and...I'll meet you
in the rustling wind
at this,
our special place."

Many a young girl's heart has broken.
As their dear lads marched off to war.
And love spilled out upon
the cold hard ground
to be lost
forevermore.

The Call of Mother Ireland

Row after row of green-suited men lining the highways and
streets. Faceless, nameless, and dangerous. Whose threatening
presence assaults each new risen morn.
Until they are become but unwanted fixtures in a house without
walls. A world with no end. And the drum beats on.

And the sun keeps coming up. While black-clothed weeper's
lower death into the ground once more, as slow mournful pipes
do play. Crying forth for the freedom that falls upon long since
deafened ears. And Bryan and Donal walk down to meet with the
boys at the local pub. To tell tales of Liam, the boy they once
knew. It was him twas' buried today.

And they'll speak of the wasted youth that's about, who have no
respect for a grand lad such as Liam. It's all so sad. Liam, like they,
were wee lads bouncin' on their father's knees...growin' and livin'
and lovin' together in Kilkarne. When livin' in Kilkarne meant
there was still some honor to be found. Not like today. When
great shoutin' s flung about and anger where there no longer
seems a cause. How many Liam's is it now who've passed to the
great hereafter? All the years of fightin'...and all when fight seems
to have lost it's meanin'. And yet another mother's heart is
broken. The breaking of a mother's heart is a religious ritual now.
In Ireland, havin' babies is almost a young woman's instant
elevation toward sainthood. For there is none more brave than
she. Walking the highways, she looks at the faces lining her
streets. Searchin' the souls of all men to find just who it is that
would snatch away in an instant, the breath of her own dear child.
And you can hear her ask time and again as she goes down the
rows of green..."Was it you, are you the one?"

Inspired by the song: Freeborn Man, by Jon Mark/David Anthony
Clark, from the cd, 'Leaving Ireland'

The Moor's Sorrow

Sorrow calls across the moor
And who will answer this fine day.
I kissed him oft' on cheeks of red
and bid him on his way.

With hugs hung tight around his neck,
sayin', "Farewell bonnie lad
now gone to war."
And looking deep through the mountain mist,
could see him there no more.

The winds they quickly go a changin'.
Brilliant blue skies can turn to black.
And sorrow calls across the moor
with n'ery a one left
to answer back.

They marched off, each one they did...all crisp
and fresh and new. To face the sting of days.
Then fell, they did...one by one, and
vanished in the haze.

The memories left of his lovin' smile,
his laughter music in my day.
The fond farewell twas' all was left
on the moor across the way.

For what's left are
apparitions, of a life that
used to be. And when sorrow comes
callin' across the moor, the one
left to answer...
just me.

The Honor Of Memorial Day

From days gone by they carried high
the red, the white, the blue.
Battle scarred, wearied, worn,
they stood side by side and true.

These were the boys who marched away
some to return no more.
Some died upon our humble ground,
some fell on a distant shore.
They were all the youngest, sharpest, best,
too young for what they'd see.
Uncertain in those first steps taken
what the price for freedom would be.

For peace could never rule the day
or freedom truly ring,
without the courageous paths they took,
and the sorrowful course it would bring.
Brave and handsome they marched away
the patriots paths to trod.
To protect, defend, with noble hearts,
their lives in the hands of God.

They were the bravest of the brave,
these soldiers we loved and knew so well.
Plucked from loving mother's arms
Into the battlefields of hell.

Loved ones left behind forever, their
boys lay now in unmarked graves of white.
There's no comfort for the families and friends,
or tender hands to catch the tears each night.

Untold griefs and sorrows.
Unbearable truths to bear.
Unforgettable lives cut short so soon,
and who of us will care?

For each boy that left soon became a man.
Each life lost was someone dear.
And every time we recall them now,
will keep them alive each year.
For they deserve not to be forgotten,
they deserve to be etched in each heart.
Teach the children and remind them often,
that good men gave their lives, for their start.

So pledge your allegiance this day to our flag,
and carry it high and with pride.
Freedom rules in our lives and our souls
because courageous soldiers have died.

•

Memorial Day Blessings to you and yours today.
And if you have a veteran close by within your reach,
grab and give him a hug and a thank you.
Offer to go with them to the memorial services near you.
And just be there for them.

•

Dedicated to my Uncle James Curtis Pharaoh WWII
Jack Morris, Korean Conflict,
All the men and women who gave their lives to God, their
families, and this country that they love.

Have You Seen Him?

(Dedicated to all the empty arms...casulties of war)

Excuse me, have you seen my son today?
Ruddy good looks, tall handsome form?
He was last seen carrying a weapon
over his shoulder.
He had a duty to perform for his country,
but now he seems to be gone.
Why is it that the useless rabble
that freely walk among the good,
and bring only pain and harm
can do so at the grand expense of
the brave, courageous, and best of our own?
I see no equity in this.
And he's so far from home.
I can not reach him. I can not go and look for him.

I think I see him in your eyes,
in a familiar stride or gait.
But it's never him that comes up the walk
when the porch light goes on at night.
My heart remains hopeful...foolishly, some say.
But my heart is conditioned to remain in hope
as long as he's away.
Excuse me ma'am, did you hear his voice?
He sings like an angel, you know?
But the only song that plays on and on
is that of memories I hold so dear.

He used to ride his bike like a bullet
to McGinty's corner store. Where hard earned coins
from a paper route brought home sweet confections of all kinds.
And always a taffy or two (my very favorite) for me, intermingled
with the violets he'd stop to pick along the curbside for a lovely
wild bouquet.

We cried together when he lost his dog. She was such
a loyal friend. And again years later when his only grandma
went to heaven to join her. He's my boy.
My pride...my world,
a world and all - away.

Please, can you look and find him?
My heart can not be still until he's home.
He is a great and compassionate, kind and loving man.
He is a loyal, proud, and strong soldier.
He is my son and he's not here,
and I need him home.
My heart needs him home.
The world needs him home.
Can someone just please...bring him home?

Today
my son came home.

In a flag-draped box so still.
No more grins from ear to ear, no more
"aw mom, you worry too much"
from the angelic face I knew and loved so well.
Only silence.
And when they say the words that "he's at rest now...at peace"
my heart breaks a little more.

It breaks over and over again...

for the very peace he could not continue to live for.
The family that he could have nurtured and grown,
had he only had that chance.
He would have been a great dad.
We could have used
more "just like him," many said.

I only wanted one.

So, go celebrate your Memorial Day by buying the
latest sale bargains at 20% off at all the 'Memorial Day Sales'.
Make sure you've extra beer in the frig and
charcoal for the grill. 'Celebrate' and enjoy the three days away
from work that you've been granted.

It all came at quite a price.

And if you happen to stop even for one moment,
to consider the lives that you have, the freedoms to live without
restriction, the very fact that you can move about and choose
how you'll spend your day on this Memorial Holiday,
take one minute to remember,
if you would be so kind...

My son came home today.

Memorial Day 2009

A few moments of silence to honor the lives of young men who were lost through the ages in battle, hardly seems enough. For they left their homes and families not to "march off to war"... as is often the poetic image portrayed, but to leave everything familiar for the strange and harsh planet X somewhere out there. Where they learned new ways to act, to think, to respond. New and foreign behaviors that often betrayed their tender ages and character. They set aside all they knew and learned to "do as they were told" and right now! For failing to do so could cost the lives of the new friends they'd just made in this foreign world of fight, or most often, even their own. Or worse than that, make their lives unlivable at the hands of a very hostile enemy where they may be captured and tortured.

Yes, a scant few moments of silence to revere the hundreds of thousands who "did what they were told," learned a new way to survive in places unfit to live, who did it because they knew it was the right thing to do, just doesn't seem hardly enough.

But even so, a few moments of your time to silently thank them for being the brave ones who did do this, who sacrificed their youth, their dreams and aspirations, their potential, their very lives, is better than the alternative (to not be thought of at all).

In the business of living life today, fully free to leave your house and drive to wherever you want to go, to choose to do whatever it is you'd like to do, take that few moments to bow your head in thanks for the freedom to live the way you choose to live your life. For the soldiers who have made this particular moment in time a possibility for you...for us all.

They were the brave, the courageous, the stalwart, the honorable, the real heroes this country has always needed. They stepped up. They gave 110% and they lost everything but the respect they all deserve so well, and gratitude of this nation. Today we honor them. And pay our respects to each one.

May those who died in the service of their country always be honored and respected and revered for the ultimate sacrifices made so that we, our kids, our grandchildren and their children know a world of freedom and peace.

Peace in the heart comes from God alone. Peace in the world as we know it, most always comes as a result of a soldier's sacrifice. We must not ever forget.

God Bless our military men and women - and may He yet bring home safely those still serving today.

Have a meaningful Memorial Day!

Our safety - their work.
Our freedom - their sacrifice.
Our lives - their gift.

And to the families of all the fallen veterans - we ask God's blessings and comfort in your lives, as you try to live on without your loved one nearby you. May you all find comfort knowing that they died not in vain. That they were very special people who we may never get to thank, but who we are grateful to, and we just wanted you to know. Your sacrifice has been the greatest one. And may you always know that we realize that fact most of all. Your son, your daughter...to your loved one lost, our pride and our gratitude forever.

God Bless.

Unexpected

Who can measure sorrow
when it comes in one small whimpering word...
"gone?"
How does one explain it, and what that really means?
The lingering scent of his presence.
The shirt he wore, just yesterday?
Phantom footsteps from his boots
on the stair steps,
that these ears still hear.

It seems it was warmer here yesterday.
There's a strangeness about the place now,
a coldness has crept in unexpected...unlikely...unwanted.
The corners once occupied and rooms filled in abundance
with the essence of him, now take on an empty
pallor about them. Odd how one notices things like the
dust on the end-tables more
at times like this.

Weren't we just sharing another life dream the other day?
My breathing space has narrowed, dare I even try
to take another breath? Surely I can't see beyond this veil
of sorrow and the tears that wash me to my very soul!
We shared. We lived and laughed and breathed each other in.
And we became life as one...not two.
We saw things the same, finished each others
thoughts and sentences, became irritated with the same
things, knew each other better than we knew ourselves.
And we shared a deeper view of eternity
than this world and all it's trappings
offered.

He went on ahead, now here I sit...
measuring and weighing each minute.
Counting tears between the memories
and the lines of life that replay like
an old 8 mm reel stuck, and
revolving over and over and over
on the timeworn screen that is my mind.
What I wouldn't give to set it aright
upon it's spindle and splice in another frame or two.
But the hands that could have stopped the turning
were needed somewhere else, and the measuring goes on.

Sorrows so profound can never be measured.
And love wounds as well as sustains,
while we live on mortal plains.
Only then to peel off the layers that keep us
fastened to this earth and venture skyward in due time.
You take no sorrow with you, it is all left behind.
And dear broken hearts left standing in it's midst
must learn to take it up and carry it well.
Until the time when it can be placed at the feet
of that One to whom sorrow is no stranger.

For only the One who has lost the very best,
who has given the most cherished,
could possibly hold the true measure
against which all sorrow may be weighed.
Those tears?...collected and counted.
That loneliness?...duly noted and felt.
The sorrow?...sustained with a promise.
He is not gone,
just away.

Written for TXRose from Pro Health Boards at the sudden
loss of her husband, Jim 01/31/02

My Sad Familiar

She and I were the same age.
She and I were engaged to the same guy. But not at the same time.
The difference was, I moved on and left him behind...and she
married him. They went on to have a little girl. They named her
Tracey. I babysat for Tracey when she was tiny.
Jane and he were divorced, and it left her a struggling single
mom. I wondered why he couldn't have been what she needed.
I lost track after awhile, but had heard about Tracey's battle with
leukemia. I would see them, her mom and her, every once in
awhile. At the ballpark, the movies. Tracey's little bald head
shining out and held high, like a badge of honor for bravery from
the terrible fight she fought.
And Jane was always there, quietly in the background.
Loving, supporting, encouraging, filling in the gaps.
Trying valiantly to be strength for her daughter.
I believed there was none left for herself when all was said and
done.

I hadn't heard anything for quite some time, but had wondered
often. Then finally I got the word. Tracey was gone. She had died
lying in her daddy's arms. I felt sad for him...and for Jane.

I had remembered enduring his pain when his sister had died
unexpectedly years before, leaving a little girl and boy, and a
young lost husband to pick up and try to carry on.
I was there.
And I couldn't imagine his pain at losing his only daughter.
And then there was Jane.

Time has a way of going on. We have a tendency to forget what's gone on before. I saw Jane once in awhile. She always had a quick smile...but her eyes were always sad.

Sometimes she'd say she was struggling, or "coping the best that she could," other times she said she was just doing fine.

The last time I saw her, she was occupied with her teenaged son's activities. I didn't even know she'd had another child, or that she'd even been with anyone else since the divorce, but I did catch that comment about how her Tracey and our oldest son would have been the same age "this year" had Tracey been there.

She was smiling and seemed happy and 'caught up'.

I remembered thinking, "Gee, it's nice to see Jane doing so well for a change." That was probably about two years ago.

I left with that picture of Jane standing there happy, in the archives of my memory stored.

Today...they buried Jane.

She and I, uncommonly tied through the years with delicate perishable threads. Our lives touching haphazardly here and there, like butterflies with broken wings trying their hardest not to crash-land in the garden of life.

I admired her. She'd been through much pain, faced fatal foes and won. Or so we thought. But she was mortally wounded, with her life ebbing away.

Jane hanged herself this week.

She was preceded in death by a life filled with dreams unfulfilled, promises broken, and a precious daughter named Tracey.

I asked and questioned, and queried and railed about this earth shattering event in my life!

God, couldn't she have overcome the pain of so great a loss?

Didn't she know that she was inscribed in the palms of your hands? Or were there too many losses that she just couldn't quite seem to recover from them all?

One thing is sure. If I ever see "Jane" again...in the neighborhood, down the street, in church, or anywhere ever again, I will never just walk away. I will reach more. Take risks. Go out of my way. For right now, my heart aches remembering what could have been.
It's too late to say, "I really do care...let's get together, let me take you to lunch." Jane's gone.
 I liked her.

She was a noble struggler who just finally
wore down from the fray.
I wish I had helped her do battle.
Maybe it wouldn't have made a difference.
But then, maybe it would have.

She and I were the same age.
She and I were engaged to the same guy.
But not at the same time.
I babysat for her baby girl, Tracey.
We had been uncommonly tied together in life
with delicate perishable threads.
Our lives touching down just now and again.

I liked her.
And I wish in the long run of things looking back, I'd been there
for her.

In memory of Jane (Eaves) Lass who lost her life to suicide this
week.
March, 2001

•

A front may be worn to be what it's not meant
but one wears it as a fool, and deep in discontent.

165

The Color of Death's Eyes

(the idea for this piece came from a message board writing prompt)

Do not linger in your gaze
as you look upon Death's pallor.
The ruination of men is seen
in depths untold
behind eyes transparent
and void of color
or hue.
And yet they appear a glowing red,
until the final blow.
And hideous monstrous neon shades,
as Death wields it's merciless scythe.
Icy fingers wrap around each heart beating
to squeeze...until it beats
no more.
And the dead and dying stare at last
into Death's frightful haunting glare.
Without mercy,
without breath,
without life,
without color,
without hope.
The color of Death's eyes
is
Pitiless.

Oh death, where is thy victory...where is thy sting?
For those whose hope is in the Lord, death is neither frightening
nor final in it's dreadful assault. It is but a mere "stepping off place"
from the familiar here and now, into the assurance of what the heart
already knows.

Sorrow

There's a particular sadness
which lays upon the heart, lingering there.
Sifting slowly down, deep below the surface
to settle.
It subtly begins insinuating itself
into the small crevices, tiny cracks,
and deliberate holes left here and there
by life's unyielding inequities and painful pricks.
It makes the mending and healing of
said heart, imperceptibly difficult, at best.
A layer of sadness laid down, one upon another,
time after time after time.
Until any bit of hope, even the tiniest glimmer
that ever sparked anew within it's precisely
beating chambers, becomes forever hidden
by a blanket of darkness...sorely felt.
And even when the brilliant light of truth
has come and pierced it's walls and shattered
this particular sadness into innumerable
scattered particles,
it lingers.
Banished into the furthermost places,
it then suspends as dust, until lightly falling to
rest again, layer upon layer, time after time
after time.
From such time worn grooves and inroads made,
an unsettling metamorphous takes place.
Of life, gravely altered. From an unkind and unwanted
infinite dark mistress whose name
is simply known as
"Sorrow."

There are things so beyond our ability to understand, that take place in lives. We are visually assaulted with the worst pictures of these daily in the news. Atrocities of all manner across this nation, and from around the world. Horrible accounts of man's inhumanity and acts of cruelty to fellow man. Tear stained and soul wrenched faces which haunt and tear at one's heart.
The tiniest and most innocent among us, whose eyes no longer sparkle, but are open wide to view incomprehensible acts and uncertain yet very real fears, played out minute by minute, in a world of deprivation and want, hopelessness and peril.
Faces that shout with desperate pleading silence from behind defeated, vacant, no longer life-affirming eyes. Void of any joy, they have long passed the one last tear held in reserve.
And then, there is the deepest sorrow we all feel from the loss of a beloved partner, family member, or cherished friend, that leaves us far too soon in life.

For this particular sadness, there is no name, there is no cure. But when HOPE can be reimplanted in a heart that's barely beating, in a life that's barely there, therein can a future be found. One raised from the ashes of sorrow. Born from a wisdom of nurture and kindness, gratitude and goodness, with love in it's midst.
And although 'Sorrow' definitely leaves her lasting and unchangeable imprints upon countless broken lives and hearts for all time, with loving care she's kept at bay. Only allowed to surface on occasion at the hints of past hurts and sadnesses remembered.

Given a firm foundation and proper care, and the right tools to help nurture it along, HOPE can grow. Even in the most darkened sorrowing hearts once again. Spend time today planting seeds of hope where you live, so that the love that follows can renovate someone else's broken heart. In so doing, you will have helped to heal the world.

Grief

There are so many things
that can induce grief in ones' life.
A 'parting' away from that which we have dreamed about all our
lives and come to realize it will never be.
Resolving our hopes and ambitions to the realities of our
circumstances of life.
Yes, we grieve most profoundly over those we hold dear who leave
all too soon.
But we grieve as well for the countless other losses we encounter
along life's' journey.
A budding ballerina grieves the loss of the use of her legs which will
no longer hold her upright.

A renowned pianist grieves the loss of a hand in a terrible accident
which leaves him only echoes of the great compositions he once used
to play, to drift down the corridors of his life's dream.
The ending of intimacy in a marriage which pulls apart couples and
leaves them cold and empty instead of close...for a lifetime.
Committed in stone for whatever reason, they are trapped in a
loveless joyless bubble "til death they do part."

The soldier who loses dignity as a result of a random impulsive act
during the most stressful of human conditions. Who has to return
home not as a conquering hero, but the shamed fallen in the eyes of
those he loves, whom he has let down.

Losses.
Each are an integral part of living our lives.
And grieving what we lose in life is something that we learn
hopefully, when we're young.

But sometimes that grief so overwhelms that there is never solace to be found anywhere, in anything or anyone.
It is all-encompassing and life devouring.

When we learn losses in small doses throughout our life, the huge monumental ones that come may not necessarily seem so much to then overwhelm us.
But when we struggle, we know that even though we feel so isolated and alone in our wrestlings with sorrow, we are not.
Every human on planet earth will have at one time or another, experienced it in some form.

Sorrow is the common link in the chain of our humanity that binds us with one another and holds us fast in kind, as one. It is the only emotion that carries across thousands of miles into tiny underdeveloped remote villages, from teeming life in New York city, to touch hearts the same.

If you struggle with loss, no matter what that loss is,
if it is hindering you from experiencing fully the richness of life that you so desire to have, there is someone always at the ready to help you through it, and you do not need to struggle on alone.

Grief is such an insistent companion to us in life, that we do well to learn to live harmoniously with it. Balancing it with the other bits of life that ground us, and keep us sane.
Getting through it's often dreadful and devastating effects and coming out stronger for it, gets us another step toward being a whole and healed human being, better equipped for the small and large tragedies that come.

Some in their grief, never lose that inner strength or the faith by which it comes.

It is that God-given strength of spirit which speaks to the grief of the one peering out from barbed wire encampments, surrounded only by death and terror and bleak hopelessness, to "go on, to not lose faith, to live anyway."

And it is that strength of spirit which whispers to each one whose loss is so very overwhelming, "you will overcome and live through this."

If you need help sorting through your losses, handling your grief, then find someone. Sometimes there's someone right next to you or a keystroke or phone call away. And there is of course the great mystery of God who, if you have read or know anything about at all, is Himself, well familiar with grief. Have you spoken to Him? Maybe nothing will happen. But then again...maybe it will.

Grieving is a curse and a blessing which builds the human heart. If you are in the renovation process from grief's' devastating blows, remember that your foundation has been set, and that one day you will see the strong reinforced end result that is a heart at peace through it all.

•

A Wise Quote from my son, Jason

There are far more important things
to be concerned about in life
than death.

(how true)

Don't Come

When I die, do not come to weep for me, now that I am gone.
What ever good could it be? When day after day, I needed you here
your life chores and personal fancies kept you away.
I was never included in your "to do" list each day.
So now that I'm gone...please, please stay away.
For if I've meant so little to you in all of my waking hours, your brief
tears of remorse at my passing aren't needed. Nor are your feigned
"too late" gestures or flowery offerings.
Do not think for one moment that you'll be comfort for those
I love, left behind. You were never here in their struggles and
triumphs before, nor stepped up in their lives to be kind. And they
acutely noticed your lack of concern for them and for me, so it's just
too late to offer it now.

No, today is set aside for those who truly did care.
Who showed the greatest love by "just being there."
So today as they lower me into the ground, go about your mundane
busy work as you've usually done. And please just don't come
around. Just let my true family whose tears are sincere, alone to weep
at my grave site today, it's not you they are needing here.

•

Tomorrow is just "too late" to convey feelings of love and concern to
those we do love. We may wake up only to find them gone. So don't
hesitate to begin to change your life to accommodate those who you
may pay lip service to only, when in reality, you know you'd just be
devastated without them in your life. Do it now because tomorrow
just may not come.

172

Today I'm Wondering...

Today I'm wondering, will I ever feel well again? Or is it only to be downhill from here on in? Will I ever have enough minutes in the day? To do the necessary, piled up and demanding, daunting tasks I see? Or the things that lay quietly, just silently pleading for a glance from me? That would be such a joy to do if only...
Will I ever have any real energy to count on again? To get me through a day without falling in a heap? Or can I make myself do the things I've procrastinated far too long, just because?

There really is no good reason that can be given for such procrastination. Because time does tick away by seconds, that too quickly translate into hours which quickly steal my day away. What will this day mean to me...to anyone else? There's a lot of wondering stirring about today. And a lot of questions about just every little thing. And the day is overcast and hazy-foggy, chilly and damp...sort of like the inside of my thoughts that fog the brain. I always feel the unrest that is CFIDS percolating just below the surface before fully launching into an all-out "flare." Ah, yes...the ever lurking "thing" that captivates my entire being and holds me prisoner at it's whim from time to time.

I ache more. I am depressed more. I move slower.
I think too much. I think too little. I think in thick and unrelenting fog that skews my reasoning all together. I don't like this. And I fight it with whatever energy I can muster. But days like this that spur the cyclic nature of the illness within, do not allow for much of that. I argue with the brain that says today we will sort, clean, toss and organize the messiness of living here into sparkling shining rooms to enjoy dwelling in. My mind wants so much to motivate the body to "get at it", but alas, here I sit. Cantankerous body dictating the entire itinerary of my day by stubborn refusal to move. I have been told that each day is really a gift from above, but today...I'm truly wondering.

The Life Macabre'

We are dead folks
Dancing at the morgue
Pretending it's the thing to do.
The time tickers ticking away.
Life is an illusion.
A farce, some cruel joke.
And not for dead folks
Like me.

I'm done with the dance
Thank you my dear.
It's time now to finally sleep.
The dark is my comfort
A lasting best friend,
But I must entrap it and
Not let it go.
For it too eludes me
And slithers away
At the dawn of every new day.

Stop the music...end this dance
Lest madness become
The suitor which weds my dark soul.
Turn loose of me life
For I can not go on.
A dead soul fraternized
With the living.
The dance has become
A pointless act, a gesture of hell's own design.
So don't knock on my door
Come the morrow un-friend,
The door is bolted securely within
Against the likes of you.
And despair has swallowed the key.

Perchance to Sleep

Ah, sweet black nothing
that is sleep.
When next I lie down
wouldst thou take me to thy bosom
never to return?

For within your able embrace
exists no pain.
No thoughts, no demands,
no disappointments.
No having to feel at all.

Blessed numbness.

I can not go there lest I am led
along paths mostly hidden
from my view.

I need say no "Good byes,"
just go! My farewells to the world hold
no meaning, and are a mere hindrance
to my longed for peace,
which lies awaiting
to envelope me
within your silken
black embrace.

And now...
to slumber.

Sinking

I swim up from the bottom.
Looking straight above me,
seeing what looks like sunlight
tickling the surface of the sea.

I'm passing through monstrous tide pools
and trying to stay focused on the outcome...the escape
from the depths of despair.
From the crushing weight that wishes nothing more than to pull me
under in the wet grip of tears shed.

In the battle for breath and sight at the surface,
I ponder where I am
and where I just came from, and I wonder if I'm lost.
Am I lost? A tiny speck in the endless ocean waters of weeping?
Center of never-never land, my only bed?
With no comfort to be found.

I try to list upon my back and just casually take it all in.
But the enormity of it all stands to become too much
without so much as a life-preserver.
And I find myself sinking...once again.
Shall I give in to the vastness of the swell? Shall I breathe and just go
down?

I think not...for I may have yet enough strength
for one more try.
Shall the waters of struggle that I flail against gather round and
overtake me?
Life is the swelling tide from which there is no escape
without struggle.
Faith is the strength that keeps this head above the waves.

God is the rescue.
In the midst of exhaustion, in the hopelessness of drift.
When night falls and fear becomes the ocean in which I flounder.
And when these eyes so swollen see no promise of starlight
in the deepest, blackest torments...
when life ebbs away without so much as a whimper.

And with the water now stilled and glassy,
a strong cutter approaches
with awesome power and purpose...
to rescue the perishing, half-dead soul, which has
not an ounce of courage left to fight against
such great odds.
And I see the long arm of deliverance reach
to pluck me safely
into the confines of it's care.

And once more...delivered, I trim my sails
to set out to sea again
with the morning mists rising in the
new day to come.
With the cutter but a few knots behind,
in wisdom waiting.
Determined.
Full well knowing all the while, that He will find me again
in the vastness of life,
in the terrors of the seas
of pain and sorrow
sinking
yet again.

The constant unrelenting pain of Chronic Fatigue Immune
Dysfunction and Fibromyalgia make for some pretty rough sailing
on the seas of life.

Add to these Myofascial Pain Disorder and a handful of other ailments, and you could say it's been a downright struggle against the gale force tempests that rage. My constant throughout the thirty plus years of illness, is the God I came to know when I was 28 years old. I know deep in my heart that for me, I could not have lived these years without that constant in life. Without the knowledge that there is one greater than myself to pull me up when I just know that I am going down for good.

And although the years grow even harder as time wears on, and other illnesses have begun to plague me along the way, I still know where the strength will come from when the navigation becomes overwhelming and out of control. The captain of the cutter is steady and sure and dependable, and there...always! And I know He always will be, even in the worst of storm-tossed life.

I first published this online at: SafetyNet Online Support Community in 2002. We are now known as the CFIDS/ME, FMS, and Related Disorder's Chatter Box at Yuku.com.

If you are struggling with some type of autoimmune disorder, or chronic pain syndrome/disease, you can always find help and support from some of the nicest folks you'll ever meet there online. You do not ever have to feel alone in the battle against serious "invisible" pain and illness. There is always someone who knows exactly what you're going through and you just need to know where to start looking.

My first advice always is to "look up!" And then seek out some friends who have already been dealing with what you are going through. These are the most understanding people because they have struggled also. And hang in there! Look for the rescue. It may take awhile to reach you right where you are listing in that sea of suffering, but it will always come. In the interim, while you wait just listing on the waves of trouble, seek out the ones who can throw you lifesavers to hang onto until your help cometh!!

Days Like These

It's on days like this I feel so small.
Like nothing of life makes sense at all.
And days like this that do drag on,
until the joi' de vive
is simply gone.
If not for but a tiny shaft of light,
there seems no hope in this long
dark night.
For which to give wings to my dreams.
I dream far less these days it seems.
My world is narrowing
and smaller still
than yesterday, which was all uphill.
Yes, days like this do make me sad
for the former life that I once had.
But when at last
my soul takes flight,
days like this
will be long from sight.
I'll run and skip and fly and soar
to heights n'er imagined ever before.
I'll laugh and sing and
do as I please,
and remember not...the
days like these.

Caught

Once more I'm ensnared.
Entangled in unbreakable
webs of agony.
I can not fight, I can not move.
I can not see.
Oh, that I could proclaim it so.
Not to see, not to move,
not to be.
But endless unrelenting pain,
has made life a mockery.

Concerning Fear

Fear, the dastardly purveyor of incapacitation.
The demonized partner of pain, which in and of itself, in one
swift motion obliterates the soul.
Please do not allow the fear that grips your present
circumstances, drive you away from your only immediate
escape route. When you speak, you conquer.
When you step forward, you have power
over those things that threaten
most.

- placed first on Walkers in Darkness Friday, march 14th, 03'
by, linda marie carlson, under the pseudonym: elle -

Walk This Way

Walk away from the dark.
It's tiring
groping for any light
just to make your way.
You do not travel alone.
There are countless thousands
all about you.
Unseen wings that gather
to quickly catch you
should you falter as you go.
We travel.
It's what we do.
And when and if we reach glorious light,
where color bursts, and beauty dwells,
the dark doth shrink away.
Light dispels dark's evil intent,
and we rarely feel it's cold again.
We're left then to wonder,
why it ever held us so fast
within it's vice like grip.
There is life and healing
in the light.
Touch the hands that are
reaching out to secure
your sure place in it.
And then just watch the
darkness peel
away in utter defeat,
from the mere glimmer
of hope renewed...
in your eyes.

Published on Walkers April 7, 2003

Life Oblique

Here in the land of the Bildebogs, in earth's core do we dwell.
Forsaken by compassion, we do linger along life's paths to hell.
For daily we're awakened to, the darkened charcoal burn
that hath held us in it's death grip lulled
from sweet life, for which we've yearned.
And stumbling we do strain to see, ere' a hint of brightened sky.
A tender morsel, a soft word extended, to pain filled hearts that
cry. From within the confines of this place, we await that moment
which frees, where hope is born and spirits lift high above the
trees.

And then leap to heights unfathomed, seeing sights to steal our
breath away. Leaving far behind the black smoked ruins that have
kept our joys at bay. For all too soon our lifetimes end in
whimpering shivering pools. Which mock and taunt with bitter
sorrows how we've lived as fools.
For at life's end is our awakening, and bittersweet the gain,
to awaken to an eternal morn, and begin life over again.
To have trudged the paths of sorrow,
and not look back to where
we've been.

For looking back brings shadows, too dark for the light of day.
The course of time moves onward and we dare not block it's way.
For all the things we've pined for, the dreams now vapor...gone.
Compel us to move past sorrow, and prod us to go on.

So move now dust that is my spirit. White knuckled struggle that
is my plight. Pull up this off kiltered life to stand at the brink of
dawn, far from darkened night. For in the netherworld we travel,
and in the day to day we roam. And we'll not rest from the
wearied journey until the heaven's hills of home.

'Life Oblique' was born from struggle. The struggle of living daily with chronic illness and the life issues that can make it so tough to get clear through to the end unscathed. We all have our crosses to bear and life can be a real battleground. For some, it can be a nightmare that never ends, and just can not be figured out.

In dealing with so many chronically ill people through the years, I have come to admire and respect their pluck! I guess in a sense, you could say we are all "survivors." Having to live our daily routines with this "thing" dogging us each and every moment.

The patients with CFS and FM and the many other illnesses that can come into a life without warning, have learned to look at life differently than others. They can soar from the highest peaks to the lowest of lows in a matter of minutes just because their bodies do not function like everyone else's. The smallest tasks can be absolutely life draining to the one who has an invisible illness. And although our paths in life are rocky and fraught with obstacles, we've learned to work around those things that beset us. We live fully to the best of our abilies and with as much gusto for life as we can possibly muster.

My hat's off to the brave and courageous men and women I've met through the years who have had to learn to "deal." Who've had to face so much just to have a "normal" routine that works for them. Who have learned to live beyond themselves to reach out to others whose struggles may just be too much for them to bear alone. Some of the greatest people on planet earth are the chronically ill folks I've met. They love unreservedly. They expect nothing in return. They live fully and live well. They are kind, compassionate, passionate about life, and they are there for you anytime you need a friend. Often when you can not find a friend to call your own from the "real or so-called normal world." And although they live the life oblique, they are the most centered people you could ever know. And this is dedicated to them all, those nearest and dearest to my heart.

For What It's Worth

I wrote this several years ago for a contributing patient at Pro Health support board who called herself "Wandering." She was trying to win her SSI award for the debilitating illnesses of CFIDS/ME and Fibromyalgia. Her attorney wanted her to put an actual monetary value on these disorder's affect on her life (as if). Well, his attitude got my ire up and so I wrote the following response as to how her attorney might possibly find a dollar value in there somewhere.

Dear Wandering,

You go call your attorney and ask him to cut off his left leg. Then his right arm. Tell him to stuff cotton in his head until it feels good and full and then wrap a layer of gauze around his eyes. Then tell him to swallow a cool quart or two of marbles to roll around and wreak havoc in his stomach and intestinal tract. Add a few hundred pin pricks to his muscles all over, take Excedrin, Aspirin, Advil, sleep help pills, anti-acids and everything else he can get his hands on and just swallow them all.

Stuff some golf balls in his shirt and P.J. bottoms, then try to sleep well through the night on them. Tell him to then go to his cronies, friends, family members, coworkers and try to tell them he's not a bit well because of all these things and their effects. Let him watch while they all turn their backs on him or tell him that he "certainly looks well enough, so what's his problem?" "It must all be in his head!"
Have him be humiliated and made to feel like an idiot because "he looks fine" and shouldn't really have all the problems he's supposedly experiencing, and that everyone with the highest level of professional expertise and experience thinks there's nothing the least bit wrong with him and that he must just be a whiney,

wimpy, complaining, lazy and doesn't want to work, sad individual. Tell him that he will now have to quit golfing, swimming, fishing, boating, tennis, bicycling, eating things he loves and used to eat the heck out of, but can't now because they may make him feel worse if he does, or even react adversely to them.
Tell him he can no longer do the things in life that he enjoys the most, the things that validate him and make him feel like a 'normal' human being.

Then and only then, would he, or could he even begin to have an inkling of what this DD (darned disease) is worth!

Tell him that ultimately, he would just have to scrap everything familiar that he knew in life and basically start over. (That would also encompass the years of hard work, effort, time and money it took to educate and make him a lawyer).

So, now he can take his gravely altered life and attempt to find and make a livelihood, restore his lost dignity, find some semblance of balance in the whole process of trying to start his life over from scratch. Then and only then would or could he see what you are going through, what you face every day of your life...for the rest of your life!

•

We suffer because of these illnesses. We don't always look like we are suffering, but we are. Just ask any CFIDS person. There is almost always constant pain. Constant mood swings, constant everything! And you lose people to the "inconvenience" of these disorders. Friends don't call anymore. Family just thinks you're crazy or mean-spirited, or obnoxious, or worse yet...faking!

These illnesses can rob and steal you blind of your vitality, joie de vive', your health, relationships, and so much! Husbands have left their wives who have this disorder (I know three right off the top of my head).

Professionals have come just short of calling patients "liars" at times, who have claimed this diagnosis. Patients are still not believed after years and years of mounting evidence that proves that CFS is more than just a psychological illness (which is what most people think), and all of it can never have a dollar value attached. How can you put a price on a life that was?

But if you venture to do it, go for everything you can and then some! And then try to just structure a new life to live while you can still live it! And never let go of your dreams! Even if they are gravely altered, you may still be able to see them realized if you just keep believing!

My Silly Reasoning

May all the eggs you lay in life
come out pointy-side first!
So that when looking back
upon them,
It won't seem nearly such
a painful experience.

The Sleep

(written for Lynne, a former SafetyNet support group member)

In the hour between darkness and dawn
behind the veil of gray, when swirls of thoughts
pervade the mind and crowd the dreams away
I wonder.
And I seem to struggle toss and turn, and reach for
things not there.
How is it dark morn fools this heart so, to think
love lingers fair.
I sigh.
Then arise with heavy spirit of purpose
alone, to make my way.
Can I in doubt and deep distress face another day?
I cry.
I know not what this day will bring.
Nor if my heart will live, to see the brightness of the morn,
or to whom my love I'll give.
I wait.
Until tis' darkened night again, and shadows hearken
round' my door. Tis' but an empty soul that slumbers...
a ghost and nothing more.
I linger.

Then awake to hope once more.

•

So many chronically ill patients lose their spouses to divorce.
Lynne's marriage was just one of many such casualties in the daily
battle for health. It takes it's toll not only on the patient, but the
spouse who may be unable or unwilling to stick it out with their
partner. When this happens, it not only breaks the already hurting
patient's heart, but the hearts of friends who have learned to share
one another's emotional as well as physical pain.

Bounced

Sucked into a vacuum,
into a vast black void.
In limbo
does my mind do it's unrest.
Am I dead?
Some days merge into others
without so much as a nod
in their direction.
All have become the same.

I feel so inhibited and strange.
So unlike who I thought I was.
Is this the canker that eats the soul away?
Or just the pause - before the illness
reaps it's dreadful reckoning?
I do not know.

Struggling, white knuckled and bleeding, as
I desperately cling to any sign of life there may be.
And there may be but a sliver left some days.
And the days wear on and on.
I seem to have no escape.
Something's boarded up the escape routes
and I am left to float forever
in this gray wretched nothing I have left.

And then the illness backs down.
Slinks away into it's ungodly realms,
a mere shadow that lurks round' my door.
And I sigh with relief once more.
Until the next time I'm ricocheted into the oblivion
that is my life
"on CFIDS."

The Gift

Some days are just like an endless summer.
I've had several actually. Those ones where you wake
up and realize that life isn't some bad dream you've been
having after all. It's real and pretty relentless at that.
Such is the case with so many who suffer silently with
'invisible illness'. Mental illness fits that bill, and so does Chronic
Fatigue Immune Dysfunction and Fibromyalgia (which some
people mistakenly equate with mental illness). You know the old,
"It's all in your head-thing."

Those who suffer these things, do so often times more deeply
even, than those with easily recognizable diseases. After all, who
doesn't hurt to the core when someone they care about, a beloved
family member or friend brings home a diagnosis of cancer, heart
disease, multiple sclerosis, or diabetes? Not that these diseases
are more visible to the naked eye, but they are more readily
recognized as being legitimate and serious.

We who suffer the horrible affects of immune disorder, in the
form of CFS or FMS, or Adrenal Disorder, or one of the countless
numbers of immune modifying illnesses, are often shoved to the
side (unintentionally maybe) by others. This includes those in
the medical community as well as people who surround us.
Loneliness for us can become a very real and heavy
burden to bear.

In reflecting back, the realization comes that somewhere
in all these years, I used to actually have relationships
with others. Meaningful ones that I thought mattered.
Chronic disease came in and spoiled all that. One never
knows the true meaning of "fair-weather friends," until
confronted with constant thunderheads and hail showers
in life.

Even family members can become a distant and seemingly uncaring lot at times. It is so often merely their inability to flex and change in situations that arise which seem life altering, that this may happen.

And most just do not have the proper understanding of what's taking place in this one who used to be 'the life of the party', the drop-everything-and-take-charge person that lives in the body they see that is so familiar, yet so incapable of doing any of those things anymore. It's a sad scenario all around.

Be that as it may, through years of pain, heartache and struggle on a daily basis, the loss of identity...who you are or thought you were, and what makes you...you, to find yourself starting over again and facing a life you don't really know, one truth stands out.

And that is what a gift your life is! Especially if it's a strong and healthy one. One where the word 'limitations' does not exist. Where you don't have to put activities and decisions on hold to think about whether you really will be able to do them at any given moment or not, or whether you can come through on a commitment made, or follow through with plans. Life is challenging. And a common phrase we often hear is that "no one makes it out of it alive." I say, "Life is challenging, and those who live a life full of love and laughter despite the challenges, live far beyond this world of trouble."

When you learn to live each day as if it were the only day that you'll ever have, and you've touched one more heart than you'd originally planned on reaching with a word of encouragement, an act of kindness, you will have lived a meaningful life that leaves something lasting behind when your time here on earth is through.

We are endowed with gifts from a God that knows us personally and intimately. They are ours to use as we see fit. To share or not to share. My constant prayer is that if there is anything worthy in my life, any gift I can bestow, that God give me strength enough to do it.

To help me to be able to look past the hurts, disappointments and pain, the lack of my own reserve, and trust that He who began a good work in me, who gave me the gift of insights learned from under the wise, yet often difficult tutelage of illness and suffering, will complete it to the end. That He will help me use what I have to reach beyond my human condition to the heart of another, who may be embroiled in pain and struggle.

Yes, as challenging as life can possibly get to be sometimes, I have (we all have) been given a tremendous gift. May you use yours in ways that will bless you because you have given, as well as received. Because you have unearthed precious treasure from underneath mountains of adversity.

And may you be able to say, " The life I live is one of discovery and underlying joy, even from behind the confining walls of pain and constriction." And may you be blessed beyond earthly measure because you received a precious gift to keep, but wisely chose instead, to give it away.
I would like to thank you for your precious gift.

·

Lift your head high this day.
For in the very act, you may catch a
glimpse of an eternal rainbow of promise
from the mud puddle you're in.

Monsters and Such

A poem I wrote and dedicated to my fibro friends in the writer's workshop I initiated at Pro Health boards back in June of 2001.

Not everyone is who they say that they are.
Not everyone is what they seem.
Many make homes in Troglandish places
And spin life from outlandish dreams.

But many are true with hearts that are pure,
And possessions of love and care.
So tread lightly oh, Troglodyte scavenging hordes,
For true love is the victor of war.

Scamper along under cowering shadows,
Seek whom to maim and destroy.
But those pure of heart with no dreams in their heads,
Can never be robbed of their joy.

For the fairies and sprites and flutterby bunch
Hide deep strength that is rooted within.
And ugly old Troglodyte monsters and such
In the end, don't you know, never win?

We who have chronic painful disorders, find ourselves often fighting discomfort and discouragement daily, which may come at us in a variety of ways. If you're one who has been doing battle of late, just remember who wins in the end.

The Never-ending Endless

I see the
grimace.
I own the pain.
I can not imagine
that endless rain.
We all know the rain...
will come now and again,
but no sunlight at all...
make dark thoughts
never end. In
the clouds,
in the dark,
where hope
seems
so small...
End the rain,
End the dark,
Before there's
no hope
at all.

This is dedicated to my cousin Chuck whom I loved, and who lived his entire life with the horrible pain of migraine headache disorder. For which there was never a solution good enough to help get him out from under the hideous pain. He lived his entire life, into his thirties, trying to run from it until the combined 'solutions' got the best of him. He died at home one night alone in his room, just trying to live. And to my niece Kay and my sister Sandra, who struggle with this almost daily as well. And to Sharon and her teenaged daughter Caitlin, who have to rearrange life every single day to accommodate this wretched painful disease. And to Megan and Gina. Each of you have brought the reality of this horrible illness home to me. God Bless you all, and may one day you be free of it. The text of this piece is fashioned after the form of a footprint. A reminder that pain's tracks left in our lives are seen by One great enough to carry us, on those days when our knees begin to buckle under the strain.

The New Day

Every day I awaken
to face a brand new day.
Good fortune could be my welcomed
guest, but I know that she won't stay.
For too often days are overcome
by the faceless cruel disease,
that storms in uninvited
to do as it is pleased.

The tears that soaked the pillow,
the loneliness inside.
Foisted upon me in such a way
that I want to quickly run and hide.

Then a gentle rush of air
brushes soft against my cheek.
An angel no doubt, reminding me
of the unseen help and hope I often seek.
I lift my eyes toward heaven
and my heart and hands to God.
He can be my strength this day
and all the days on earth I trod.

The illness unrelenting, can
never steal my soul.
It can never take the love inside that
has healed and made me whole.

I am not this wretched illness!
I will not let this thing reign!
I will keep my head held skyward
until I can stand again.

No more room for sorrow,
sorrow is exiled here.
I have a mansion of expectations
free from pain and fear.

God, I thank you for this new day
to rise up from the ruined remains.
Thank you for the strength you give
when in shadow sings hope's refrains.

Living It Anyway

Why some must suffer an entire lifetime without a morsel of
relief, and yet others glide effortlessly through is far beyond most
everyone's understanding.
Some say "God makes a difference," and indeed a difference He
does make. But it's not always so noticeable to the human
condition-life's circumstances. The difference is in the abilities
given, at His own discretion, for handling what comes. That inner
strength that allows the embittered, embroiled-in-the-battle-of-
life mere human being, to stand up under the most dire of
circumstances imaginable. Pick themselves up, dust themselves
off, and move forward.

There is no rhyme or reason to it, no "figuring it out." But there is
a rhythm of life, which when interrupted, demands the mighty
hand of the one who has it all in His hands to bring about that
precise cadence once again.
So often I write from the perspective of one trying to live in that
skewed rhythm of life that I face with chronic illness, and from
life's circumstances that have led me here. I suffer physical and
emotional pain from these. Depression from years of doing battle
on both fronts. Intrusions into life that have led to hours of
pondering the "why's and wherefores."

And occasionally it has found me desperately pleading for "better consideration" from a loving God, only to come to this; that sometimes there is just no solace here on planet earth. No relief. So, we'd best set about doing the things that we can do, the best way that we can do them, despite that fact. When relief does not come, and pain rules our almost every waking hour, we learn to stick a permanent smile on and grit our teeth and go for what we can anyway. We grab every ounce of joy and life and laughter that comes our way, and run with it! Through the pain. We are going to have the stupid pain anyway, so why not instead of suffering even more by just sitting or laying there feeling every teeny tiny minute' sting of wretched illness, force life out of the depths of suffering while we have breath to do it? Live anyway.And live
in such a way that we'll have lived to the very fullest best of our ability to the very end...pain, suffering, and all? We'll have at least been able to, by so doing, take the fond memories of life (albeit somewhat altered maybe) with us when we go.

I'm holding life hostage!
Until the body catches up with it. And I am going to get on with the business of living on through the struggle. When you're "one of us" (chronic sickies), you know it's just what we do. We take a new slant on life, close our eyes, step up and start breathing once again. Remember we are ill not dead as long as we have a breath left in us. Yes life is or can be, one gi'normous pain! But we need to determine fully to live it just the same!

Dedicated to all my (SafetyNet) Chatterbox-Hob Nobbery, On A Clear Day, life-affirming buddies. And anyone who pushes through the muck to try to live life anyway. And just F.Y.I. I want you to know that I could not take another step in life without God the center and source of the strength it takes to do so. When I can no longer feel the ability to push, He pulls (me through). And the friendship and support of good online friends sure hasn't hurt either!

The Number's Up

I'm too decrepit and old. There's nothing left of me anymore.
The good I could have done is all too left undone. And it echoes
down the hallways of empty regret. It is said that "youth is wasted
on the young." Perhaps that's true. Just ask any child trapped
within the confines of two-wheeled push chairs peering out from
behind the wrinkled masks now worn. Or from behind too quickly
dimmed bright and hopeful eyes. Deep within there lies the soul of a
ballerina who has yet to dance her 'Swan Lake'.
Or a young soldier who replays over and over again, the greatest
victory of his glory days. His being away from home the very first
time on the shores of Normandy doesn't hold a candle to the battle
raging within a tired body that can no longer move.

For all their dreams, hopes, and expectations from days gone by,
have somehow lingered in the midst of time's ravages, leaving only
a slower beating and yearning heart. Bittersweet memories evoke
waves of emotion that call out "what could have been" but never
was. Too late in life we are left to discover the way things should
have been. And too early in life do we then die, to awaken in the
morrow' of eternity only to begin again.

It Only Hurts when I Laugh

It only hurts to sneeze, but then, laughing is no breeze. And
taking a step or two can knock the pins right out from under you.
Then there are the times when I do actually manage to move. Making
this old needle feel it's skipped a groove. So when asked "how are
ya?" by the well intentioned few, I smile and say, "just dandy...and
just how's every little thing with you?"

I Miss My Life

The one that I must have lived.
I look back and see children, for just a fleeting
moment. Dogs and kitties and cub scout meetings
and tricycles. So busy, and so very short the years.
Who was that woman that really had no idea
that all too soon it would fade into some long ago
and far and distant land?

I know I didn't dream it.
There are pictures that show
that it was real - once upon a time.
But the faces small and round have grown now,
into limited and occasional chats in adult lives
that are far removed from what "used to be."

And growing old is hard.
And fading back and moving away is lonely.
And who was that vivacious, living, breathing, long-haired
conquer-the-world woman, who became the wistful, saddened,
sorrowful soul that sits here pondering now?

I miss my life.
The one that I know I had.
The one I'd love to travel back in time to, and grasp
with all my strength of soul and take with me, into the
coming unknown days. The quiet eventless days of grays
and shadows. Where thoughts wander back to brighter times,
to the fantasies of what I'd like to have been. For my children,
my family, my husband, and for me. One can never travel back.
One can't undo things long forgotten by
everyone else but me.

But there's also a hopeful heart which stirs within me
simultaneously. When I think of heaven and what's
to come. Maybe then, when there are no more tears,
no more sorrows and sadness, I'll see me for
who I really am. And a merciful God will let me
start again.

I'll do it better there. And I'll love longer,
deeper, truer, and be more worthy of the
love bestowed upon me in this life I used to live.
For the love I've had, although scarce,
has come as a pure and lovely offering.
A gift that sometimes was foolishly
left unwrapped and sitting on a shelf.
Who was this foolish woman who
did not accept
such wonders offered?

Yes, the days grow long and I grow weary.
With a far too quickly lived life
that was hardly even there
before it moved on.

I wish that I had noticed more.
I wish that I had loved well.
I wish that I had chosen all that was good and right.
My wishes would not serve to let me grow old
in grace, or let me have much in the way of peace.
No real purpose do they hold.
And now, looking back at all that's been,
truly, I miss my life.

Lift Off

O Lord,
I want to shed this skin.
I want to leave this crazy world behind
and light upon your footpath there,
upon Thy hallowed ground.
To touch the innocence of
new born wings that never
chanced to fly.
To embrace all those unreachable
things which life would not allow.
See beauty for what it really is,
where no ugly deed remains.
Take me up to your special place
O God, I cry.
That I may breathe your promise,
that I may see your face,
that I may live
far away from these evil days
filled with cruelty and pain.
Please equip me with the
wings I need
to just lift me
off the
ground.

•

Serve me quick death upon the dirt floors
of meaningful thatched-roof huts,
not slow agonizing life served upon golden
china, behind empty palace walls.
- lmpc/2000

Invisible

I am the invisible woman.
The windowless room with no view.
Others paint the world vibrant colors,
I am void of color and hue.
Beautiful others without effort, do grace
each corner of life where they glide.
I watch and yearn for such beauty to share
but shrink further away and just hide.
I realize I've nothing to offer.
A mere afterthought am I.
Yes, I am the invisible woman
blown on by the wind
with a sigh.
- 2006 -

•

I am the vapor.
The unseen mist
which occupies this house.
Ever untouched by human
compassion.
Where once dwelt brightness
in every room, now merely
resides pale shades of gray.
How quickly we fade from life's
beginning of promise,
into dreamlands forgotten
so far away.

No Regrets

Haunt the hallways of regret. See the discards where
not a sign of life shall stand if one lingers too long there.
For the past is just the substance from which knowledge
and wisdom come. And the mistakes back then, the building
blocks, where new beginnings then come from.
So frequent there if you must, but then leave it far behind.
There are those who become ensnared in it's memories
most unkind.

Look ahead and glean life's lessons, from amongst
the memories stored. The trinkets of mankind's struggle
strewn where God met man in one accord. There's healing
around the corner as each dark sorrow you release.
No need to fear the "letting go," from your surrender will
come strength's increase.Strength to take you through
tomorrow,away from the harmful and sad.
Replaced with newfound peace of heart, that you never
knew you had.

So haunt the hallways of regret,
but from it's rapacious walls then run.
For lives built upon it's foundations crumble,
hearts that linger there too long, chance to
become broken and undone.

The Book

Empty rooms
and empty hallways.
Chairs that sit
where chairs always do.
Framed pictures above the sofa,
fringed lamp that lights the settee
where once life danced around.
There now lies silence.
Surrounded by familiar walls.
Life begins so innocently.
And meaningful 'things' fill houses, so
as to furnish a home.
But my life is a book.
With only rifled pages
never fully read.
Closed,
with dusty cover.
Never revealing the me that
dwelt only in my dreams.
Where one resides
but does not live the true
passions of the soul.
But ends up unopened,
lying upon the table with
no reading glasses to be found.
Within the empty rooms and empty
hallways
of a life once lived there.

"Vanity, all is vanity...a chasing after the wind"
- King Solomon in Ecclesiastes

Life Spent

Lock me in a chamber and play sweet music there.
For life has passed too quickly, and I no longer care.

If a gift of life is given to be squandered and flitted away,
by the time it's reached it's very end what is there left to say?

I'm sorry...I didn't get it...I knew not what to do?
The deaths we die so long in coming, reveal so little of the vast
eternal view.

Glide we blithely through our days, filled with meaningless
endeavor. Stopping briefly to catch real beauty, rarely, if almost
never.

For all we live in fairyland in the deep recesses of our minds.
Creating our own good with our own designs, with little regard
of mankind.

Selfishly we plunder on to reach our selfish end. And what have
we to show for it? What great chasms did we mend?

So lock me in a chamber and play sweet music there.
My life has passed too quickly for anyone to care.

•

"...only what's done for Christ will last."
(and in the end at death's final call, love is the only thing that
simultaneously travels with you, and is left behind to live on).

•

Minute by minute - hour by hour,
elusive life scatters with the wind.

Metamorphous

Chiseled in stone.
A cold hard end to a long
endured agony.
No cherubs or angels
nor floral tributes.
Just rough hewn marble
void of any sentiment at all.
A slab aptly descriptive
of a life without purpose.
Here lies the physical body
of a soul now freed to live.
For death was the agent that
cracked open the shell
containing the real person
no one ever saw.
Then wings took over
and lifted skyward
to finally let her feel
she
belonged.

A New View

If you took your troubles to bed
with you last night and used their dark
clouds of turmoil as your cover
from the cold, I hope that
you'll awaken with sunshine
streaming through your windows
to bring you a sunny outlook
for the brand new day!

Touchpoint

Chaos, destruction, dearth and depression
in the midst of all.
Beneath the soft bleak soil awaits
rebirth.
The earth rebels,
it's people mad.
Time spins out of control.
The dirge plays on and on, and yet
beauty lies.
Anticipates it's time to come.
In abstract union,
birth and death.
Evolved knowledge's of
unthinkable life.
Littered here and there with
human rubble.
Little thought of how things
should really be.
And so, the breaking forth new
ground.
The tiny living green to grow
and carry on the plan
of life's precious petals
touching
stone.
Amid the hurling Godless realm,
a perfect rose has come and
touched my heart.

Written in or around 1977 and submitted to World
Poetry Contest. It received an honorable mention.

Blooming Random Acts

I did not grow up with an abundance of acts of kindness or tenderness in life. Not that I recall anyway. And, not that I didn't experience any somewhere along the journey to adulthood, but just probably not any that I could consider life-altering. So needless to say, it's difficult for me at times to know just what to do with them now, should they arrive in some form or another, almost fifty-two years later. Much of the kindness I feel towards mankind seems to fall short of what I've seen or experienced from others, and leaves me feeling quite inadequate in the random acts of kindness department.

Last summer I read a heartfelt plea of sorts, in the form of an editorial from an eighty-something year old woman, who had been the victim of the thievery of some lovely ferns she'd had sitting outside of her apartment building. It had evidently not been the first time the poor woman had been victimized in this way. Her question at the end of her editorial asked, "Why would anyone want to steal an old lady's plants?" After reading it through two or three times, I just couldn't get past that question. Why indeed would anyone want to do such a thing to a harmless elderly person whose only joy and passion in life at this point was the pride she took in her flowers. I imagined that she had gently tended them and treated them individually as precious living things that in kind, rewarded her with bright beautiful foliage and colorful blossoms that burst forth in sheer appreciation for the kindness being offered them.

I set about calling the newspaper in which the article appeared. I wanted to find out where this woman was located. Of course they could not divulge such information, so I started investigating. Several phone calls and a walk through the telephone directory later, I located the address. I then visited our local green house to pick out just the right fern (since this seemed to be the object of choice of the plant thieves).

I found a huge full plant that was lovely, and I chose a flowering something or other just to ensure color and brightness enough for the moment that would speak and possibly say, "not everyone is like the plant thieves in life," to the woman.

The ladies at the greenhouse knew exactly where to send me, as they were familiar with this particular housing area. I had at first wanted them to deliver them to her, but none of them could for various reasons, so I set off.

On the card enclosed I wrote, "Jesus loves you"... with her name placed beside the words, and the sentiment that it was hoped that these would brighten her day. When I arrived, I was greeted by some of the loveliest flowers I had ever seen. And I knew that these new plants would take their place of prominence at home with the best of them and thrive. She answered the door and I asked her name. When she confirmed that she was the lady in the article, I handed her the plants and said, "these are for you, and that I hoped she'd have a nice day," then left. The whole exchange barely lasted three minutes, but I left there with a lighter heart than earlier when my day had begun.

I knew that she'd never know who sent the plants. Maybe she thought it was a friend or relative, or perhaps she thought it was a guilty and repentant thief, or the flower shoppe itself of which she very well could have been a frequent customer, from the looks of her little garden. Whatever she thought, I was thankful that I was able to have a very small part in trying to restore some faith in the kindness of others in a world where it seems the exception, not the rule.

No, I may not have had much experience with tender acts of kindness through life as it were, but the most tender act of kindness was extended me many years ago from a heavenly Father that loved me enough to open a world of brilliant and radiant blooms from His garden. And now I can share bouquets every once and again with the world around me. All I must remember to do is ... look beyond the weeds.

Flash

There was a smile there just the other day.
Mysterious in origin. Impish in nature
on just a moment's whim.
In a flash!
I know I saw it.
And the moment was recorded
for the next all too gloomy day.
Filed away for perhaps another time
when just a flicker of momentary joy
would be most welcomed.
Too quickly did it dash to hide behind
the walls of stoic every other day.
But it will still be there in reserve
just waiting
it's rare appearance again to make.
Should the moments of sorrow and struggle
work to try to crowd it out...
in one split fraction of time,
just when least expected
it will be there.
As if in possession of some
ancient secret joy
which spurs it on
in an otherwise mundane morn.

•

Even Ozzie and Harriet had a real life!
- lmpc/99 -

Simplicity

From stars and birds and trees and things,
it's simple beauty that makes hearts sing.
The noblest of kings upon the earth
can n'er bring riches of such worth.
Can not ever capture joys of the
smallest and best,
such as a soul that is loved and a
quiet place to rest.

As we travel life's byways with heavy
loads to bear,
our blessings will come from other's hearts
that care.
And all of the riches and all of the gold,
can not wrap you warm
against bitter cold.

Contentment can never be found in those.
They leave one lonely, in want, and exposed.
Wonder of wonders, quite astounding and yet,
the good simple life lived,
leaves no longing
regret.

Life Chapters

Yesterday my hubby, our youngest son and myself, went to look at an acreage. Now granted, most people our age are looking toward retirement and a move to town. We on the other hand, look to "escape" to the country. And the solitude of the quiet breezes blowing through the trees, and cricket's orchestrating their latest symphonies in the quiet night air. We are just two people who have known nothing more than the noise and commotion of living "in town" since our marriage almost 33 years ago.

Not that it hasn't been nice. It was convenient for raising our active children and scooting off to any number of assorted school activities from a short jaunt up the street. And if you ran out of milk, you'd simply run to the local grocery store and just pick up a half gallon when necessary. But we have decided that the reclusive life that is afforded one in the beautiful surroundings of a country home sounds inviting at this juncture in life. Most everyone would probably "pitch a fit" to know we were even considering such a thing at our age. But it's something we've wanted for quite awhile now, and I think at ages 52 and 56, we're "grown up" enough to decide on our own.

The house we looked at yesterday was beautiful. It made 3 of our present home. It was enormous. As you pulled off the gravel road onto the long driveway, it made quite the visual impression instantaneously. It reminded one of the grand homes of the south. Four great white pillars commanded ones attention and demanded recognition as soon as the turn was made. The yard surrounding the home was perfect. Perfect trees, perfect flowers, perfect!!! And although we didn't think we were going to be able to get in to see what treasures lay waiting inside to complete our visionary delights, our inventive realtor found a way in. (the daughter of the owner had forgotten to unlock).

Well, as we virtually watched our realtor, a wonderful christian man who is as honest as they come, slip through the window into the garage, our anticipation grew.

As he unlocked to let us in, we were not the least bit disappointed with what we discovered therein. Huge amounts of natural oak woodwork lining every nook and cranny of this house, which seemed filled with dignity and character. Time worn wooden floors, which I'm sure were the ones that creaked as you walked across them at night throughout, it was lovely. I envisioned my writing room here, a bedroom there, each new turn sparking new and innovative thoughts as to how and where we would place the "stuff" that makes it more than just a place to sleep, that makes it a place to belong. Every corner of every room seemed to "speak" that this was a very special place.

Eventually the owner and his wife showed up. Both elderly, they had lived in this house 56 years. Raised two children there. Lived a full life together right where we stood. Mr. Swanson's wife had Alzheimer's. She flitted about in her surroundings while we were visiting, asking her "Merv" if he'd seen "mother" about, and upon receiving a negative answer responded, "well, we'll just have to find her and tie her down, won't we?" with a big grin on her face. While the men visited in the yard, I watched her go pick up a tree limb and carry it off to the small grove at the side of the yard. I observed her in these surroundings that she knew all so well.

While her thoughts were in a far off land, I saw her tiny frail self go on "autopilot" in a place that seemed so comfortable for her. Before we left, we received at least two hugs from this beautiful little lady, who I'm sure was quite unaware that we may well be the very ones who would remove her final connections to this place I was certain she had loved so long.

As I left, I had many thoughts to be sure. How would I, with the chronic illness I suffer, be able to manage there? Would I be able to manage so well as this little lady? Would I put the effort love and care into making it a place of solace and peace for the backside of life for us to enjoy, as much as she had devoted her years into breathing much of the same in the frontside of life for her own family? There is much to be weighed and mulled over before ever committing to something so permanent and monumentally big. It may never come about at all. We may keep looking. But I walked away from there seeing not just the aesthetics and beauty that had been obvious immediately, but seeing and coming to appreciate, that it wasn't a house, but a home. Some dear persons home that had been tended and cared for with years of love and devotion, and memories attached that I couldn't begin to fathom. And a subtle reminder that life is filled with living changes all about.

Life chapters is a continuing story that contains many many different characters, that is being continuously rewritten and added to from one life span to the next. With a multitude of sub plots, beginnings and endings, and twists in the story. I know this much. If we do end up there one day, there is an unspoken heart's promise to Mrs. Swanson, that I will love it well, and try to breathe the same passion of living into making it 'home' as she was once able to do. And there won't be a day pass, that I don't picture her there.

•

Here we are some eight years past this story, and I sit amazed at the chapters that have been added to our lives since it's writing. We never did buy the house, although I would love to have lived there. We now reside with our son in a beautiful old renovated church in another community altogether. For now, it's what works for us all. And I will continue to add to our life chapters with every new one following in place after another. Just as they're supposed to, until the final epilogue is written. And if you ever find yourself house hunting, remember to look beneath the surface of all the decoration and fancy trimmings, to the "home" that lies within, it's own life chapters to tell.

The Watcher

In darkness doth dwell Golgolith.
Amidst moss green blanketed
palisades and red ferny fronded shoots.
Velvet green valley's do beckon. Wispish and
breezy soft as a whisper in the wind.
Glance quickly.
For a glance is all you'll get.
Of toady brown jumper's
and dewy water skimmer's hurrying to their
appointed rounds.
But Golgolith haunts and hides in shadows
seen only as mists. See him upon yon mountaintop
or in the shallow meadows there.
The watcher of all things. The ponderer of unknowns.
Lumbering and silent he makes his presence known.
To wee birdie chirpers and low earth gliders
and fluttering things with wings.
And to leaves clapping time with earth's rhythms
and life's melodic score.
And just how is it that all creatures do dwell
under the shadow of the most high?
As Behemoth and Leviathan sport about
nothing escapes his eye.
Blossomy brilliant colors unfold sending sweet
fragrant incense about. And Golgolith awakens the world from
it's slumber, to strain towards the heavens
and touch God's own hand.
Who in His great wisdom created all.
And all that hath life praise Him.
Look on O Golgolith, and stay your post.
And watching, await the dawn of a new heaven and earth
and the coming of our King.

Garden Cat

I think today that I shall stroll
along the garden pathway.
I might spy a butterfly, or
mousie friend at play.
I know the birdies will be there
at the ready for a tussling,
and little bugs that dash around
I'll investigate in all their bustling.

So many sights and smells and sounds,
for my kitty eyes to behold.
As I walk the garden pathway,
my adventure to unfold.
The garden sights hold treasures,
too many for kitty paws to count.
And wonderful kitty pleasures, amongst
the beauty strewn about.

My little ground squirrel buddies,
the squirrels up in the tree.
I know will all be poised to play
at the very sight of me.
So today I'll stroll the pathway
of this lovely garden sweet.
And I'll relish each new step taken,
warm beneath my feet.

For each little paw print that I leave
will a glad reminder be,
that joy sprung from my little romp,
with my garden friends and me.

(A prompt from a writing forum)

Summer Prayer
From A Winter Heart

Narrow the days of discontent
and broaden the simple wonders.
Still the clamoring soul within
that worry the days
And keep the nights awake.
Needing so, the beauty of life
In a world disheveled with pain.
Shorten the sorrows
Which imprint the heart.
Reveal the sun
Which will end my rain.

Columbine

(placed on Yuku Profile, Monday, april 16, 07 the day I wrote it) along with a picture of the blooming purple Columbine from our back yard pond.

Oh,
the sweet
fragrance
of Columbine.
Lovely to behold.
How is it that you've been
laid so low?
A dark blight's attempt
to extinguish your beauty,
and yet in sunlight you raise
your bowed and saddened heads
to remember that today...
you bloom eternal.

For the students, faculty
and families upon this, the
eighth anniversary of
Columbine's darkest day.
April 20th, 1999.
Our thoughts and prayers are
ever with the families of
the children slain this day,
as well as the students and
families of Virginia Tech who
were killed by a madman
Monday April 16th, 2007.

Light Play

I could have sworn I saw the moon
bounce up, then rest lightly
upon the ground.
A sly grin across it's face, eyes laughing
without a sound.
And the elfish glimmer that flashed
as it gently romped and played,
just warmed my heart so
I skipped upon the light trail
that it made.

The still world awash in the glow
of mischievous moon's fun time.
Captured for but a moment of chance
a moment most sublime.

Yes, tonight I thought I caught the light
of Mr. Moonbeam's glittering glow.
And enchanted, I fell into the warmth
of it's beautiful moonlight show.

How quickly envious befell the stars.

•

Music is a byproduct of the depths of
human emotion.
No song was ever born without feeling
or purpose.
Just listen, and tell me otherwise.

Autumn Life

Fall comes, and thus the slumber.
Rest from long and busy summer.
A dying back from long labor's days.
The world becomes most colorful just before
it's wearied journey ends,
while a new season yet awaits it's beginnings.

Gather the beauty of the day.
While birds still soar and the fields are ripe and full.
And do not keep the sorrows gleaned, but empty them
fully, alongside the harvest of life's treasured days
while you may...
that they may be blown with fall winds as chaff,
far away.

And may you be reminded of the bounty of colorful
joys collected, kept silently within your heart
as blessings, when you face the oft' cold and
barren winters to come.

Each season brings it's share of lovely things,
as well as it's hardships and sadness. May the
enchantment of this season carry you through
whatever struggles there may be in the wintry days
that may lie ahead
to lift and warm your soul and keep your heart
content.

Cider Days

The chilly but beautiful fall days that are upon us have sparked a few memories that I hadn't thought of in some time today. One of the best is of time spent with our friends, the Nebbe's, in years past, making pressed apple cider at their home when our kids were younger.

Doug and Peggy were wonderful to always invite a yard full of friends when it was apple pressin' time each year, to share in this fun and happy event. And beings they owned the local bike shop business, and Doug being the very inventive genius that he was, had come up with a fine way of combining the love of both these things at this time of year. He did this by rigging up a bike to pedal the grinder wheel of the cider press, so as to make it easier to churn the red and yellow juicy fruits into pure unadulterated nectar fit for kings.

People who had their own, or had access to apple trees, would bring baskets full of the crisp, juicy, just right fruits to pool together into huge piles. Everyone would then form an assembly line of washers, inspectors, and spotters, who would cut out any questionable areas and then fill up the hopper bins while Doug (well, most of the time it was Doug), peddled the bicycle he had hooked to the cider press grinder gears, which then ground them into apple pulp, squeezing out the juice simultaneously. Sometimes one of their three boys or one of our two would hop on and ride until they just couldn't push another peddle forward, and either Doug or one of the other visiting cider enthusiasts would then take over.

Pears were often thrown into the mix, which then changed the flavor of the finished product to something akin to heaven's own nectar straight from above and we would have tasters aplenty filling their Dixie cups right out of the barrel, just because they couldn't wait for the jugs to be filled and capped off!

The kids played, the people gathered and worked together. Laughed, caught up on every local news happening and then some, and even sang choruses and a hymn or two once in awhile. And at the end of a blissful time spent enjoying the weather, the freshly made cider, and each other, everyone who participated got to take home a jug or three of golden brown apple juice to stash away in their freezer to take them through the winter months ahead, and enough good memories to last a life time as well. It was wonderful!!

A few years back, Peggy lost her battle with cancer. It seemed she had contended with it for many months, but there just weren't enough days left for all of us. We just didn't have her with us near long enough. The world became a sadder place without her. She was a dear, dear person.

She reminded me so much of "Ain't Bea" on the Andy Griffith's Sheriff of Mayberry T.V. show. She had that quiet strength and comical point of view on things that just endeared her to all who knew her. She introduced us for the first time ever, to making apple cider. What a fun and wonderful new experience! And she was an accomplished and talented choir director at our church, and a long time friend. She's the one that pushed and prodded me through the years to sing a solo for the very first time. After all, "I was good and people deserved to hear it! Ha!" I laughed at her reasoning, but by golly, it was because of Peggy that I found the courage to give it a try and then proceeded on to become a regular soloist in church and even in endeavors such as the community's yearly cantata's and fun musicals through the years that followed. I sang for weddings, funeral and special services, and became a real songbird of sorts, at her encouragement and direction.

And I remember the very day that Peggy called me over to her home to share a very exciting bit of news for the very first time ever with someone.

She had become personally acquainted with Jesus Christ, and in ways that I knew that she had never experienced before, and she wanted to share that wonderful news with me. I laughed and cried with her that day, knowing that she had received a wonderful and lasting eternal gift to share with me, that will stay in my heart's memory forever.

The last time I got to see Peg was at another friends funeral. He too had succumbed to a battle with cancer and it was heart-wrenching. When we greeted, she gave me a very long and meaningful and lasting hug. And I just knew right then, that it was going to be my last one from her. I went home and cried. That was one hug that I can still feel today! Her warmth and love came flooding through that hug as we stood on the landing of the church stairs that day, and I will never forget how it made me feel. It was her "good-bye friend" hug to me.

All the wonderful things, the things that made Peggy so special were wrapped up in that moment for me, and I still have trouble believing that she's gone and miss her yet today.

I know that she is now in heaven directing a glorious choir and I have no doubt, sipping apple cider with the angels, and being the busy bee she'd always been while here with us. And while the leaves here turn and drop gently over the still green grass outside my window, on certain crisp and brilliant Autumn days, while they dance in the brisk fall winds, I can almost hear sweet singing being lofted above the trees.

It's then I remember the beautiful Cider Days and Autumn memories. I know that I'll keep those precious memories of the more happy and simpler times we all spent together turning apples into heavenly cider, singing, enjoying bits of life's treasured moments together, forever in my heart. And I know too that one day, we'll all gather together and do it all over again.

Autumn's Gentle Fall

The autumn leaves have all stretched skyward.
And burly wooden trees begin to yawn,
anticipating the long sleep to come.
Their last "hurrah" of summer,
they bid farewell to feathery tenants
and furry trespassers, all in readying
for a chilly winter's nap.
Slowly they begin to blanket the ground
in colored splendor, as they gently fall
from their branches to cover the pathways and
tired grasses all around. And there do little creatures
sport in them, as they go about their business
of gathering seeds and grain.
Some blown there, and
some carried by fine feathered crop dusters
in their varied take offs and landings
from here to there.
Regal limbs press upward, as if in silent praise.
In celebration
of their soon coming long awaited rest.
Their time has come to shower the changing
season with leaf falls and
seedling drops.
Then under winter cold and snowy white,
they'll wait for the sun's warm calling in the spring.
Until they're beckoned once again to awaken.
How easy comes autumn...
and how lovely to be able to silently
observe it's peaceful passages.
And then come to realize,
there's a season of
change that yet awaits me.

Shy Autumn

Every lovely summer's end
awaits shy Autumn's beautiful beginnings.
Where flirtatious beckonings toward
a winter's glance, shan't go unnoticed.
She shakes and sheds her comely leaves in
an innocent taunt that beckons, "come hither"
which melts cold winter's heart
for just awhile.
And winter holds back his thunderous bluster for
but a short time, to see fair Autumn
revealed just a bit more.
And she dances within the meadows
and frolics down the hillsides
and hides amongst the leaf swirls blown
by a gentler kinder wind.
Until at last exhausted,
she lays down her head to rest.
And silently she'll sleep,
not knowing Winter's watch has covered
and wrapped her warm,
to safely keep underneath his
soft blankets of sparkling white.
To slumber then...until Springtime
paints her world and calls her awake
once again.
Blithe and lovely Autumn, do you wonder?
Could you be loved any more?

•

By now you're probably aware that Fall is my very favorite
season of them all. And winter is a close second. But then there's
Spring, and of course Summer. Hmmmm...it's just nice to be alive
and savor the beauty that every season brings into our lives!

Wondrous

He is breath that guilds the mountain sides
white with wintry bluster at the exhale.
He is silence.
And He keeps the winds and
hides the sun,
to make the glittering snow.
And yet there is only tenderness
in this gesture of His might.
The small creatures scamper
with coats that keep them warm.
The birds plump their feathers
and bristle against the cold.
And He provides their warmth
even where seemingly,
there is no warmth at all.
How marvelous the season
that births a glorious day;
when God provides
great wonder, in such a
quiet gentle way.

Snow Song

There is nothing else
like the silence
of snow falling.
No instant calm
that quells a troubled heart
quite so well
as a bleak evening tide
illumined by
brilliant sparkling gems
of white.

When all the earth lies
in darkness, in slips the snow.
To quietly dispel the long shadows
of night and blanket the earth,
as a mother who tenderly draws the
covers up around her sleeping child
to protect them from the cold.
When day's busyness has ended
and the last light put to rest,
Go sit beside the window and listen,
to the sound...of falling snow.

Snow Smitten

The hillsides were flawlessly painted white
sometime throughout the night.
Silent beauty befalls the wintry valley.
It is absolutely still.
There is only white shimmering
glitter-bedecked blankets
to wrap the earth up in.
A hushed creation almost gasps,
from the sheer wonderment of it all.
One forgets the bitter cold within,
when such beauty fills the soul.
It is a snowy heart that watches
winter at it's play.

•

Still.
It's the smallest of words that claims the greatest peace of heart.
When the world seems all blanketed in white and everything is
quiet, peaceful, and new. There is a certain calm in the spirit that
comes with the beauty of a peaceful winter's day. May you draw
the solitude of this peaceful day in, and keep the stillness of heart
that results, with you always.

Cold Spell

Some people have a very hard time with winter.
I find the fall and winter months some of the loveliest (for the most part, anyway). I love the changing of the seasons and all that goes with it. Life is all about change. And the changing seasons are the subtle reminder of that fact. But I realize too, that change can create a sadness sometimes from a cold and desolate place in our souls, what we might call, "the winter of our souls" that may linger long past the season of spring. After the snow has melted away and been replaced with the first Crocus that blooms at the hint of spring warmth that comes...the winter of the soul can linger on.

That lonely and hollow place that winter's discontent blankets around our hearts from deep and unseen sorrows, heartaches, losses and struggle, may well move in and decide to stay on for a spell. So many smiling faces may be walking on the sunny summer beaches with the lingering chill winds of sadness blowing within. Being stuck in a winter of the soul is a far more difficult season to try to endure.

So now when I see the beauty of the fallen leaves over taken, with the quiet and gentle fields of white...or the chill becomes a bit too much and I find myself shivering in the cold, staring at the barren limbs and hearing the haunting stillness over the hillsides, I anticipate that after this time of winter rest, will come a warming of my soul again. And an awakening of the hope that's in me. And for those of you who find that you're still in the middle of that chilly winter's wind, from a possibly long and burdened season of your soul, a reminder that the sun will come and warm you still. I have never known the sun not to rise yet. And even from under the clouds of a gray winter's day...it patiently awaits it's time to brighten your pathway and lighten your footsteps on your way into a sunny warm season of hope renewed.

LinQuotes & Etc...

Although I've slipped in quite a few of my quotes/thoughts throughout the pages of this book here and there, I have a few "leftovers" that I'll just place here. Not all that important or significant for sure, but just a few that didn't want to be left behind.

MY LIFE OBSERVATIONS:

Little snippets here and there
of 'life pieces' scattered everywhere.
Gathered through the years could be
a portrait of what's really me.
(I write on this scrap piece of paper here, that random thought penned over there. Half the time they get thrown out with the trash never to be connected or even thought of again. I've probably thrown out an entire lifetime by now.)

•

Wounds
There is no wound so deep as that which comes at the hands of those we love best

•

Clueless
He said, "I don't get it."
She said, "It's as clear as day."
He looked toward the window and said,
"But it's midnight."

•

You can argue all you want to
whether the glass is half empty of half full.
I just know, we're out of milk!

The definition of a writer should be
'one who wonders'.
The imagination. The inner-vision.
The passion for just...more.
When one ceases to wonder,
for all intents and purposes,
life is effectively over.

•

When asked what I wanted to be when I grew up, I'm quite certain that the first response that came to mind was not "a writer." More so, as is the case of many a little girl, my answer was probably, "a fairy princess", or "a mommy"... or perhaps I wanted to be a great doctor, teacher, an actress...but then, in sorting it all out, they are all tantamount to one and the same.

Living Palimpsest

We are walking manuscripts.
Bearing years of edited life.
With rewrites, revisions, and edits
from time and circumstance.
In complicated phraseologies
and pellucid lines that rhyme...
and those that don't.
A co-authored work by God and man.
Permanently recording who we are
for all time, and offered at no cost
to a world who considers us but
a brief insignificant read.

Words
penned thoughtfully over blank pages
small and overlooked,
spelling out life-altering thought
to the possible one heart
forever changed at their answered
beckoning call to...
"Enter"
•

There are many things by which we are bound
in our human experience.
One of the greatest of these common links
that we share is
suffering.
There is no greater wisdom shared
than that which was purchased
with the great price of suffering.
•

Teacher, your job is to teach my child.
My job is to let you.
Me, my job is to raise my child.
Your job is to let me
•

The greatest teacher in the world,
is the one who sees beneath the rough surface
of this handful that we call "child."
And then sets about freeing the precious gem that's
embedded deeply within each little soul,
so that the world may see
their sparkle.

A Limerick - is a light humorous verse of five lines
with an aabba rhyme scheme:
ROVER
(one of my lame examples of a limerick)

I once had a good dog named Rover.
Who liked to go sniffin' the clover.
But the honey bee's got him,
Stung, buzzed, and besot him,
Now Rover's clover sniff days are all over.

•

A Haiku consists of three lines. It 's a Japanese form of poetry.
The first line has 5 syllables, the second 7 and the third
has 5. Traditionally, Haiku's subjects have to do with nature. Here's
an attempt from me:

Awash with the sun
The meadow came tumbling forth
To fall at my feet.

•

Our emotions so often "take leave of their senses"
when tragedy strikes. Taking off on a whim
of their own. It's best to stay calm in the midst of their
lunacy, until our hearts are again beating their proper rhythm
and our heads are no longer twisting around in circles.
Wait for the one good day sandwiched amongst the bad,
and then break out the picnic basket!

•

Never fail to say "I Love You" when the opportunity presents itself.
It may be the last words to echo in another's heart if they don't get a
chance to see another tomorrow.

Remember Me

The sails are trimmed and open as the ship sails from the shore.
It carries precious cargo, all our love forevermore.
As she sails on to the Master, through the quiet glassy sea, her call
will long and linger...my friends, remember me.

Remember me, oh, remember me. As she sails on to the master, oh
friends, remember me.

In the times of love and laughter, in the sorrow, tears and more.
Through the good and bad and in betweens, while anchored to the
shore. By His hand she's freed to sail on, from the tether of this life.
Towards eternal sunset's beauty...freed forever now from strife.

So remember me, oh, remember me...while sailing to the Master
oh friend, remember me.

If ever there were kindnesses or good that has been done. And
precious memories stay behind of our laughter, love and fun...
then set your mind upon these things and this, my final plea, as I
leave this shore forevermore, my friend...remember me.

And when you pass the gates of splendor,
when it's your sea to sail upon,
we'll meet in the gardens of heaven,
and it won't even seem that I've been gone.

We will wile away the hours, of endless eternity....
but until then, my dear old friend...would you remember me?

Glimpses of Mom

I am including these things because they were written by my mother, Vida Marie (Setzer) Pharaoh, who passed away on May 8th, 1964. They are my sole possession and have not been copyrighted. I have full proprietorship over them and wish them to be included here in my own collection as a way of preserving her legacy to my family. She was a wonderfully gifted pianist, soloist, musician and poet. She was born and raised in a tiny town named Peru in Nebraska, to Frederick Wirtz Setzer and Katy Mabel Josephine (Carter) Setzer. She lived there until moving with the man she married, my dad, Charles Wilbur Ellsworth (Pete) Pharaoh, and their children, my siblings, to Boone, Iowa. She remained there until her death at our then home at, 1328 Tama Street. I had just turned fifteen years old a month and a day before my mother's death.
For Mama.
•
This first one was published in a Nebraska newspaper, quite possibly out of Sterling (although I'm uncertain as to which one it was for sure), in which a distant cousin, Mary Packwood, served as editor for many many years. Mary was married to Mike Packwood and was the adopted daughter of my great aunt Harriet. My mother wrote this poem for the Christmas of 1947, and the hand written copy I own carries the simple title, 'Christmas 1947' on it. It was published in the newspaper as 'Mother's Meditation' by V.M.P./ Peru Housewife.

Christmas - 1947
by: Vida Marie (Setzer) Pharaoh

"What's cookin' Mom" are the words I hear
as the door bursts open and two heads appear.
One boy twelve the other ten,
one half of our brood - my little "men".
What fun it is, this being a mother.

At Christmas time or any other.
So many things for a family to do.
Secrets to share, and not just a few.
Gifts to select, tree to trim,
somehow my eyes with tears grow dim,
as I think of my childhood, another tree,
and my mother doing these same things for me.
Oh! Yes! Mothering can be fun.
And how nice with the day's work almost done
to have your grown up daughter come home and say,
"I'll do the rest mom, you've had a hard day."
Evenings are best with my loved ones near,
and I pause meditating long enough to hear
smallest daughter who says as she stops her play,
"Mama, I made you something at school today."
Then there's much tiptoeing and sh-h-ing around
as the boys bring gaily wrapped packages down,
putting them under the tree, saying,
"Don't you peek, Mom. This is from me."
How lucky I am, the mother of four.
To be living where there's so much more
of the things that make everyday life worth living.
The feelings of friendship, the spirit of giving.
And I thank the good Father, in heaven above,
for that which I have
all the bountiful love.
This beautiful life, and the heart to say,
Merry Christmas to all, hope you're happy today.

The Pharaoh Family Pie

One handful of forgiveness, One heaping cupful of love,
A pound of unselfishness, Mix together smoothly, with complete
faith in God. Add two tablespoons of wisdom, One teaspoon of good
nature to flavor. Then...sprinkle generously with thoughtfulness.
This makes a wonderful family pie. One complete pie will serve any
size family.

A Flower Story, written by V. Marie (Setzer) Pharaoh

SWEET WILLIAM loved a girl and her name was MARI GOLD. He
needed some one to sew on his BACHELOR BUTTONS. He went to
see the girl he loved and ASTER to be his bride.
She promised she would and after saying, FORGET ME NOT, he
started home. She ROSE early on her wedding day at 4 O'CLOCK,
and gathered the MORNING GLORY for the table. The color of her
dress was VIOLET and she wore dainty LADY'S SLIPPERS on her feet.
JACK, IN THE PULPIT, performed the ceremony and the two
POPPIES and mommies (and grammies and grampies) wished them
much joy and hoped they would LIVE FOREVER and be happy .

Untitled

How often I have wished to see
myself as other people see me.
If I could meet myself some day
walking along, carefree.
I wonder, wouldn't I stop to stare?
And sorta' laugh at me?
'Cause here I am
built low to the ground.
Never could grow up,
just seemed to grow round.
With a queer and somehow comical face,
never one to be handy with
ribbons and lace.
And yet again I stop to think,
why worry about outside self? Even tho'
I know I look
like something out of a comic book.
There's always an inside left to see.
And I guess I'll have to be satisfied, for it's plain as can be...
that one can't change although we'd all like
to be a beauty instead of a fright.
There's one thing plain as the nose on my face,
I'll always be me.

Peru, At Twilight
I love our town at twilight
with lights all dim and low.
When soft balmy breezes whisper
and fireflies come and go.
Of course, I love it at dawning
when the birds their carols sing,
and 'Miss Day' awakens from sleeping
with a hint of the longed for Spring.
Then again at night time
with shadows passing by.
When 'Mistress moon' in all her splendor
comes to ride the star-flowered sky.
For me there's an hour made for dreaming,
and tis' neither morn nor night.
But the place and time that I love best
Peru, in the soft twilight.

Be Happy Today
What words those are
and yet, with the Christ Child
as your guiding star
look at the children you meet on your way,
faces shining with joy, at work or at play.
And a "Little Child Shall Lead Them" are
some words I recall.
So let's face the future with courage
and take heart one and all.
This old world of ours isn't hopeless
however it may seem.
Remember folks, we who live here
should pull as one big team.
With our hearts in their right places,
our shoulders at the wheel,
each doing his best...we'll never rest,
til' our world's on an even keel.

A Wife's Wish, by: Marie Pharaoh

Just to be beside him, just help to guide him
Just walk or ride with him, along life's weary road.
Just to be near him, just where I can hear him,
Just share a tear with him lifting the load.
Just to share life with him, sorrow and strife with him,
Be more than a wife to him on life's weary road.
Just traveling on my way, helping drive cares away,
By being bright and gay. Lightening the load.

(she was a brand new newlywed when she wrote this about the love
she had in her heart as a young wife)

•

Sort O' Miss You, by: Marie Setzer
(written when mom was still in high school)

Sort o' miss you when the dawning
paints the house tops o' the town.
Sort o' miss you when the yawnin'
sun sets in a flaming gown.
Sort o' eases all my troubles,
wakin' memories that seem
Just like bright quicksilver bubbles
flittin' though a twilight dream.
Sort o' yearn to hear you talkin',
sort o' long to see you smile.
Sort o' sad we can't be walkin'
down life's road another mile.
Sort o' little pain keeps wakin',
makin' everything look blue.
But it's not my heart that's achin',
for I gave that all to you.

* My thoughts: This is probably my favorite poem that mom had
ever written that I have. First, it was written when she was...

very young and still in school, and makes me think of when I was young and writing out of a young heart's experiences, and also, makes me wonder who she was missing. What happened that they couldn't "walk down life's road another mile?" She obviously loved someone in her young life and experienced a broken heart from it all via a 'parting of ways'.
It also reminds me that she was a young girl with strong feelings and emotions, as well as youthful hopes and dreams. She was a real living breathing human being, a young woman who had her own ideas about life and where she was going, and what she desired most out of life.

She never did think too much of herself, I do know that. She had scrawled the nickname, "Fat costello" on this hand written piece, along with the words, "my other name" beside it...then crossed them both out. She also had written the name "Toad" over a picture of herself that I have, so...I know she had the same insecurities as every other young girl growing up in the world.

Even though I'd give anything to have had a chance to know "the real mom" and have her with me all these years, I know enough to realize what a wonderfully important person she was, and still is in my life today so many years later. And, she truly mattered. Even though she may never have truly realized her worth. She gave me the equipment I have today. The ability to reach in and share through words some of my (and her) God given talent. She instilled a love of nicely penned and beautifully orchestrated words from the time I was very small, that have carried with me throughout my life. She would sit and read to me classic and lovely poetry from the past that I still remember in part after sixty years. And the time I had with her then, though fleeting, was valuable beyond measure to me for a lifetime.

Thanks mom

Thought Review, by: Marie Setzer

When you sit alone at evening
and thoughts of the day roll by,
when you think of all the things you've done,
and heave a tired sigh.
Will a little voice within you say
has your days work been in vain?
Didn't you help brighten a gloomy home,
smooth away a little pain?
You've called a cheery greeting
and smiled a sun shiny smile.
Warmed somebody's heart with sympathy,
hasn't it all been worth your while?
Why! You're feeling rested already,
albeit a little bit proud.
With a feeling of kinship to God you'll say;
Twas' a day without a cloud.

•

My Mom and Dad, by: Marie Setzer

Folks! I've got a wonderful mom and dad.
And I think you'll all agree,
when I get thru' spielin' my little piece
that they sure mean a lot to me.
They cared for me through childhood,
worked hard and sent me to school.
So that I might learn a few lessons from life,
along with the Golden Rule.
Then when I grew up folks, and
married the "only man"...
and the road sometimes was a little rough,
who gave us a helping hand?
Why! I think you ought to know that
without my counting three,

Twas' my old mom and dad, folks...
still watching over me.
So people criticize the young folks of today,
for not appreciating their mothers and dads.
Well say, I hope they'll read this little piece
and keep it on the shelf,
cause' I'm sure they're all mistaken
Because I'm not so old myself.

•

This next poem was written by mom and given to and dedicated to
her grandma, my great grandma, Sarah Carter. It was given to me by
my great aunt Harriet (Aunt Hattie), who had saved it, along with
the other memories, which I'm sure great grandma kept for years
just because they meant a great deal to her. It's pretty old.

Untitled
by, Vida Marie Setzer

If I can be as good a Christian woman.
If I can be as brave in times of stress.
If I can have the courage and the patience,
the kindness and thotfulness.
If on this road of Life which we must travel
I can see some good in every little clod,
and gladly lend a helping hand to others
who need to find anew their faith in God.
If I can make the many friends that you did.
Keep their love and faith the long years thru.
If I can live the Golden Rule in my life
and apply it in everything I must do.
Why then when at last it's time for Him
to close all earthly doors...
I'll feel Grandmother dear, that in some measure,
I've lived my life
much as you've lived yours.
Then when it's time

to close life's earthly door
and opportunities for service end,
I'll feel Grandmother dear,
that in some small measure
I've proven myself
a true grandchild of yours.

(I never knew my great grandparents, nor did I ever know my
grandpa Pharaoh. But I can get a real picture of the kind of woman
great grandma Carter was through the eyes of my mother. I'm
thankful that she had someone so wonderful to try to emulate in life.
And to evidently honor her whole life through. And mom, if you
happen to be looking in...I think you've more than "proved"
yourself a worthy granddaughter, daughter, wife, mother,
grandmother, woman, and friend. And through these things,
I know that you loved God, setting the stepping stones for me to do
the same).
•

We come from a long line of poets in our family. As far back as this
next one which was written by my great uncle Roy Carter. Aunt
Harriet's and Grandma Kate's brother. My mom's uncle. It too, was
given to me from among the "saved treasures" category of Grandma
Carter's stored memories from Aunt Hattie.

Untitled
by, Roy Carter

Pretty maiden on the beach
for the air
dressed in style most becoming,
I declare.
In a bathing suit so neat.
Dandy sandals on her feet.
In 1000 different ways
she was there.
As she sat upon the sand
getting air.

Everyone who passed her by
sure did stare.
Sitting there demure and sweet,
to look upon her was a treat.
From the bottom of her feet
to her hair.
As she sat upon the sand
getting air,
a calamity befell her unaware.
As she got upon her feet
some one hollered
"Get a sheet"...
for there was an awful rip
you know where!
•

and this one, also from uncle Roy entitled:

A Roller Skater
by, Roy Carter

A slip, a rip,
she cut her lip...
Next time she'll do better.
A slide, a glide
the skates were snide,
they proved to be a fetter.
No more she'll soar
the rink all o'er
Because her ma'
won't let her!

Poetry From My Boys

I thought it would be good to include a few things here that my boys wrote when they were younger. I asked their permission first, of course. Mainly, so that they can see that the 'writing bug' is something that often bites early on only to return years later, when possibly reflecting upon their own earlier days. I hope they will both realize their full writing potential and put it to good use some day.

They are grown ups now with busy lives that don't allow for much contemplation of life's deeper meanings etc. But one day they may sit down and have words just begin tumbling out into surprisingly insightful thoughts that they too may wish to pass along.

Here's to the written word and the wonderful worlds contained within them! And to the lives that they encompass by the mere laying them upon parchment for all the world to read. They let us imagine, make us feel deeply, transport us, commiserate with us, enlighten and help us to learn. And they let us fully appreciate life through the eyes of hundreds of thousands of others, by pricking our hearts and our consciousness, and awakening us to our common likenesses and shared humanity.

So if you have a word or two to share...
pick up a pen and write your world!

Trees
by, Jason Wade - age 9

Trees are the kindest things I know.
They won't hurt a friend or foe.
They just stand there
big and tall.
They hold back the wind of fall.
That beautiful tree
is for all.

Springtime
by, Chad Michael - age 13

When Spring comes around once a year,
I sit and watch and admire the deer.
The ladybugs and butterflies
all seem to amaze
my little eyes.
When I sit by the cool stream,
I lay my head back and begin to dream.
And I think of all the marvelous things,
my "Dad" above has made
just for me.

•

Father above, fill these two young lambs, I pray.
Holy Spirit guide them every day.
I love them more each day, it's true.
How blessed my life, these gifts from you.

The Book
by, Chad Michael - age 13

My life is like a book.
In the past, in my futile attempts, I tried and tried
to write my book.
But I couldn't get the wording just right.
Then along came a man who helped me very much.
I thought He must have been a publisher and asked Him,
but He said He was an author just like me.
So from then on, I didn't write on my own.
For I left it all to Him. This author, as I know Him,
would be pleased to write anyone's book, if they
just asked Him. Jesus?

One Lone Skater
by, Chad Michael - age 13

One lone skater on an icy pond.
He glides in such a graceful manner, such as
not noticing the crowd.
He slowly but gracefully carries out His
performance until finally...
one small boy steps out on the ice.
He stumbles at first, but the one lone skater
holds him up and helps him all day long.
Slowly, more and more people stepped onto the ice
as they found the skater has time and love for everyone
who just takes that first step.

Forgiven
by, Chad Michael - age 13

I like to be forgiven
with no dues to pay.
I like to be forgiven,
with my sins
all washed away.
To live in perfect harmony
with the Holy Three in One.
And I know when the day is over,
I am forgiven.

(chad wrote music for this on his piano and played it. One could hear
it often drifting around the house when he was younger)

In A Poet's Eyes
by, Jason Wade - age 13

The world is harsh,
the world is wrong.
People 'shoot down'
other people's song.
But there is a light in the night
for those who don't see eye to eye.
It's everlasting shine brings love
for those who hate
and do stuff wrong.
He lives in me,
A poet's eyes.

The Name On The Stone
by, Jason Wade - age 16

Names on a stone. That's all that's left.
"Who's this?" A passerby asks.
"A traveler of life just passing through,
now finished with all his tasks?"
Where is he now, where did he go? Is
he in heaven or down below?
A mystery man nobody ever knew.
But he's paving a path for me and you.
If he can travel death's long road
surely so shall we.
Many have gone on ahead, death holds
no fear for me. Death was swallowed in victory.
1 Corinthians 15:54, and 1 Corinthians 15: 15-58

Another Day
by, Jason Wade - age 16

She laid in bed with so much pain, but yet she tossed a smile
my way. A loving grandma she was to me, only...
how much longer would she breathe?
Please grandma, don't go! Please stay.
I want to love you...another day.
To laugh and giggle with you once more, I would pay a
million dollars or even more!
Cancer is such a bad thing, it took my grandma far away.
Please grandma, don't go. Please stay. I want to love you...
another day.

•

Jason wrote this for his sophomore English class on death and
dying, four years after he'd lost the only grandma he'd ever
known in life that he loved so dearly. It was dedicated to Mary
Margaret (Shaeffer) Carlson, a beloved grandma and friend.

Afterthoughts:

The boys maternal grandma was Vida Marie (Setzer) Pharaoh
who, like their Grandma Carlson, also died a long slow and
painful death due to cancer in May of 1964, almost a month to
the day of my 15th birthday.
She was a gifted musician and a poet. I know she would have
been so proud of Chad and Jason, had she been here to see and
be close to them growing up in life.
I wish they'd have been able to meet one another, but
I'm certain that one day they will meet in heaven. And that
they'll also reunite with their beloved Grandma Carlson as
well.

I hope they will continue to be able to write in life. Not only
the painful things, but the myriad's of life experiences that are
unique only to them. Sharing joy and laughter, triumphs and
failures alike.

Life is fraught with joys, happy times, frustrations, heartaches,
disappointments, and countless numbers of hopes and
dreams...and many other things that get locked away in our
hearts.

The only important lessons learned in life are the ones we've
fully lived through first hand and survived to tell about them.
The only truths that are real are those that are kept deep
within the human heart and soul. Sharing what we know is the
only true vehicle of education that exists today in it's purest
form. One doesn't need a degree to teach the lessons of life, or
the things of real importance. They just need a heart willing to
'let go'.

Life's circumstances have molded and shaped me into who I am today. I do have a loving caring family that mean the world to me.

As a young misplaced girl, I didn't have the understanding that I do today concerning how things played out in my life.

My family had very young children of their own to raise, and bringing in a disoriented young teenager to influence their own children at that time, just may have proven to be too frightening an experience.

After all, they were hearing only bad things from a selfish woman who's only purpose then was to rid herself of this unwanted "object," and she was fabricating some pretty convincing "whoppers" and making them sound believable.

I struggled back then. And even some today, as a bit of the residual fall out has sort of tried to"dog me" throughout these years.

But on the whole, I am far more able to understand things about that time, and about myself, from the process.

I'm getting well into my senior citizenry, and have tried to leave the past where it needs to be left.
Only occasionally can a certain incident trigger an emotion from "the bad old days" that has to be dealt with.
I have learned though, to quickly process it for what it is, leave it and move on.

Life is difficult. There are frustrations, disappointments and hurts throughout. And if you have these early in life, it can either help or hinder you in finding a real life somewhere in it all.

I am thankful for the love of my family. For God's inexhaustible care and strength to endure.

And also for being able to put into words some of the necessary thoughts and feelings to make it to where I am today.

I am a daughter of heaven, a sister, an aunt, a wife and mom, and friend who can relate to others hopefully, with more compassion and with genuine concern.

I am a survivor. Of heartache, loss, chronic daily illness, depression and pain...and of life.

The wanderings of the heart have come full circle now.
And the ponderings over my life have culminated into this, a deeper peace in my soul. God given, well earned, and I'm hoping...useful to someone.

Our days are short.
And learning to live life well is the most important thing we can do for ourselves. (I learned that from a very wise thirty-eight year old not long ago).
So in closing, I just want to wish you traveling blessings as you navigate your own life's journey. And may all your wanderings lead you home.

linda

A final offering...
When I realized late in the year that this book would not be published as I had originally thought in 2009, but carried over into the new year, I decided, upon my final proof of the manuscript, to include the very last thing I'd written in the year for 2009.

I include it here because it was born of an enormous struggle with a grief that was difficult to bear in my life at the time, and still is. The loss of a precious person in our lives, my sister-in-law, Joyce Marie Pharaoh. I still find it quite difficult to accept the fact that she is gone. She died four days before her and my brother's 50th wedding anniversary. She was only 67 years old. She was a precious gift to her family and is missed more than anyone could ever know.

The following is my final offering for this book and is dedicated to her and my family. It is called, "Candle In The Window." For Joyce:

Candle In The Window

How often I had gone by the house at 349 South 1st Street in our former community, the town we raised our children in. The one we left a few years ago, to move down by the river into a small neighboring community with our son. I had visited there often. For in fact, this is where my older brother and his sweet wife lived for fifty years. She, as a small child born and raised to live there, my brother, as one who would fall in love with a young teenage girl, eventually marry, build a successful loving life with two children there for those fifty plus years now.

Folks around town all knew and loved them. After all, she was a homegrown girl, a town sweetheart & daughter and he, their adopted son who had married into the community family, to then build and spend a lifetime together. And theirs has been a whirl of a love story! No one could quite fully grasp the love that had been shared between the two over those many years together.

Joyce spent her time completely devoted to "her Jerry" and their two kids. She did everything for them and because of them, and he loved her for it. Indeed, you would hardly ever in those fifty years, see one without the other. Many many loving memories were built by their four hands. Eventually, their two children grew to three with the addition of a loving son-in-law. Yes, they have lived upon their little corner of the world dedicated to one another and their little community for many years.

This year, Jerry lives on there alone. Our beloved girl, Joyce...succombed to a dreadful infection acquired after her second open heart surgery in October. She'd suffered a rather severe heart attack at the beginning of Labor Day week end, and was rushed to one of the larger capitol hospitals. She came through that first surgery all right and had made it home to then begin her recovery. She had called me about a week and a half later, well...closer to two, and in her very frail but hopeful and upbeat small voice, thanked me for being there and my concern, and her final words to me were, "I've got a ways to go, but I haven't given up yet." I hung up the phone and cried. She sounded so small and like she'd been battling very hard on this new road to being well.

I had put off going to see her because she just didn't need all the company, and hubbub of activity right then I didn't think. My intention was to wait until she was feeling stronger and more like talking so as not to wear her out. I can't remember exactly what day it was that they rushed Joyce back to the same hospital because a raging infection had been detected at our local ER.

But when I heard my brother say she was going right in for surgery, I was very scared for her. I asked him if he wanted us to come and he said it wasn't necessary, the kids were there. After her surgery, it was touch and go for many many days. The second day after surgery, we went to see her.

She'd had to have dialysis again, like after the first time, and she was on the respirator and couldn't speak. She barely opened her eyes, but once in awhile. We stayed the night and slept (along with my brother and niece) in chairs in a waiting area. The several subsequent times we visited, she would still always be the way we left her the time before. We would hear about her saying a couple of words in between times when the respirator was out, but it would always have to go back in and I never did get to ever hear her sweet little voice again.

The times we were there, I would always tell her we were there in the room with her and ask her if she knew we loved her very much? She could nod an affirmative answer and sometimes squeeze my hand. But at 11:30 p.m. on October 30th she lost her hard-fought battle. We had just been down for the day and not home all that long when Jerry called to tell us. My heart felt ripped from my chest at that news and the realization that I would never again, this side of life, ever hear her lovely voice or hear her joyful laughter again. I hurt so much for my brother, my niece and her husband and my nephew...and for us. What an enormous loss. One that still has us struggling even now.

Joyce's specialty in life seemed to be bringing about joy! Joy to her immediate family, her extended family, her friends, her neighbors, and every person that had ever had the privilege to know her. To say that she is missed, is not fit wording enough to even try to explain just how much.

One way she brought about her special brand of joy each year was to illuminate the corner of 349 South 1st Street each Christmas season with candles meticulously placed in each window of their simple but stately old two story home. Along with a beautifully decorated tree filled with white lights and silver and gold ornaments.

Her stairway bannister was always draped with greenery and white lights that you could see from outside along with the tree as well. The front porch was festooned with green pine and white lights with big red bows, and the side yard sported two mechanical deer in front of the two evergreens toward the back of the yard.

The moment you pulled off of the main highway into this sleepy wintery little community and drove past the filling station just off to the side, you'd see it! All the loving work put into bringing joy to the world for all to see, by her own hands (and of course, Jerry's as well). It was a time honored tradition through the years, and everyone I know who lived there or happened to be passing by on their way to their own loving family holiday gatherings, would always always look for this beacon of joy and light as their indicator that indeed Christmas had officially come. That it was time now, to try to set aside the hustle and bustle, the anxiety and cares, the struggles and worry, and just take in the peace that seemed so illusive during the busyness of the season for so many. It was indeed, a season of light. That the warm welcoming glow from these candles placed lovingly with so much care, were a reminder that love glows from within.

That it is not just found in gifts under the tree, or the painstaking effort that goes with making Christmas "special" in so many small and big ways for our families. It is found sometimes, by the caring act of just one...offered to the world.

It was so like Joyce to do this not just for her family but for all who would see. She knew the pleasure that others gleaned from something as simple as lighting the way for those harried travelers passing by. The instant calm and peace that had a way of just flooding into the heart at that moment in passing.

This Christmas eve, my brother and his little family will be taking a single candle out to the cemetery and placing it on Joyce's wreath as their Christmas gesture of love and gratitude to this beautiful woman who graced all our lives and touched so many hearts in so many wonderful ways. And as the town grieved collectively our great loss with us, I know they waited and wondered. Will they ever see those beautiful Christmas lights ever again?

Jerry and the kid's indication that they are going to make it, that they are going to be all right, came by way of their honoring the loving tradition started so many years ago by Joyce. We're all going to be ok, Jo. Peek out from behind that cloud and look! You can't miss it! There on the corner, shining out for all to see...you'll find that your love light lives on. And that peace of which I spoke, so illusive, can be found once more by the candles sparkling as brightly as ever. Lovingly placed there by those you've left here to carry on the task for you.

And if you look just a bit to the north, you'll see an extra one or two. For the very first time ever...shining brightly right here as well. They are my own loving tribute to what you've begun. And they will be my tribute from now on. My own welcoming light for whatever weary traveler may happen by.

I thank God for you. For the strong family you loved so much and taught your particular joy to through the years. For your way of reaching farther than yourself to touch more hearts than you could ever have possibly realized.

I hope that Jesus has somehow let you in on just how many by now. And that He's shown you that the legacy you left behind lives on and will, for years to come.

And that legacy of love can carry on for anyone anywhere, to warm just one single aching heart, if they are willing to light just one spark of hope by placing their own...candle in the window.

God Bless your Christmas.
If you ever doubt that something so simple can touch a multitude of hearts so deeply, then you haven't met the people of Ogden, Iowa and it's surrounding communities. Joyce was loved beyond measure (as is Jerry and her entire family), by a community who truly was touched by her loveliness and the person she'd always been and for her joyful attitude and loving spirit. Jerry and the kids, and we who loved her deeply, thank them all for the loving gestures made and continue being made on their behalf.

And if you ever get there at Christmas time, and happen to drive by the house on the corner of 300th block and South 1st, you will see what we've all come to anticipate year after year, as the "official starting point of the Christmas Season" right there in the shimmering candle light.

May you be filled with the peace of heart that only the true meaning of Christmas brings, and the joy that comes from knowing that love shines on, over-shining even some of the world's greatest heartaches.

•

Joyce Marie (Miller) Pharaoh August 2, 1942 - October 30, 2009
Daughter of Loren and Bertha (Ellsberry) Miller
Beloved wife of Jerry (November 3, 1959) and mom to: Lori & Jim and mother-in-law to Randy.
Loving sister and sister-in-law, aunt, and friend.
Forever in our hearts and forever loved.